So, You Want to Write!

So, You Want to Write!

HOW TO GET YOUR BOOK
OUT OF YOUR HEAD AND ONTO THE PAPER
in 7 Days

ANN MCINDOO

Published by Elevate, Charleston, South Carolina.
Member of Advantage Media Group.

ELEVATE is a registered trademark and the
Elevate colophon is a trademark of Advantage Media Group, Inc.

Printed in the United States of America

First Printing: July 2006
ISBN: 1-59932-022-3

Most Advantage Media Group titles are available at special quantity discounts for bulk purchases for sales promotions, premiums, fundraising, and educational use. Special versions or book excerpts can also be created to fit specific needs.

For more information, please write: Special Markets, Advantage Media Group, P.O. Box 272, Charleston, SC 29402 or call 1.866.775.1696.

Dedication

♥ *To my dad, Jose Cruz Figueroa, who always said, "If you do what you love, you'll never work a day in your life." It's so true. Thank you, Daddy! You are an extraordinary father.*

♥ *To my mom, Esthela Figueroa, my hero, my very best friend, who always told me, "You can do anything you want," and gave me the love and encouragement to do it. I love you, Mom.*

♥ *To Maggie Griffin, Jocelynn Rodriguez, Adriana Jones, my beautiful, loving sisters and best friends. To Otis and Troy for loving my sisters with such a pure heart and creating a beautiful family. And to Michael Figueroa, the best little brother in the world. I love you all.*

♥ *To Billy, you have a special place in my heart. You inspired me and gave me the seeds to create my writing garden. Thank you.*

Table of Contents

Acknowledgements

There are so many amazing people in my life that I could fill up 1,000 pages. On this one, I want to acknowledge and thank:

My team: Kristy Poehlman, trusted and dear friend who always takes care of me. Vincent Smetana, whose fingers fly like the wind to create beautiful transcriptions and format manuscripts. Bea Donatelli, who makes exhibiting at events an outrageous and always profitable adventure, I'm so glad we're cousins! My beautiful cousin, Olivia Walsh, who makes my Writer's Boot Camp logistics so easy.

Glenn Plaskin, best-selling author, brilliant writer, friend extraordinaire. Thank you, Glenn P, for all your encouragement and endless humor—you make writing so much fun.

Tony Robbins, big as life, with a heart bigger still. What an honor to be on the Creative Team and what a privilege to assist on your magnificent book. Thank you for teaching me and showing me a way to teach others. A grateful thank you to Sage Robbins, who has always been so welcoming and made me feel like family.

*Bobby Ruiz, who walks his talk and lives Ironman **every day**, not just on race day. You are an inspiration and an example of living an extraordinary life to its fullest.*

Loren Slocum, my nominee for the Extraordinary Women Hall of Fame. Thank you, Loren, for always making "Can Do" a hero and for your many gifts of the heart.

My amazing crew pals who have always cheered me on: Judy Osuna, whose words are magic. Mimi Gabriel, whose smile and loving energy fills up a room. Carol Grove and Linda Kedy, always sharing their gifts. Elizabeth Vargas and Bella Luna. Johnnye Gibson. Jan Walker. Michael Morningstar – always at the ready with a special elixir and who has given a new meaning to living healthy. John Burgess, big heart and helping hands, thank you for being my angel.

My savvy business coach and dear friend, Yolanda Harris, always creating the incredible and sharing a wonderful friendship.

All the authors I have worked with, each one of you sharing your knowledge, making my life richer. Thank you for adding new distinctions to an amazing process and making it even more enriching for the next author.

Adam Witty and Ben Toy at Advantage Media Group, you guys rock! Thank you for a fabulous publishing journey!

And, of course, my little Scruffy dog, who napped under my desk, missed many walks and waited patiently for me each night while I worked on this book.

From my heart, thank you all! Annie

Introduction

Congratulations on your decision to write your book! Deciding to finally forge ahead on a book writing mission of your own is a major decision and an even bigger commitment. I am delighted that you have chosen my materials as a guide post to creating a vision of your own. *Thank you.*

The three questions I get asked most often about writing a book are:

1) How do I get started?
2) How long does it take to write a book?
3) How many pages does my book need to have?

In a nutshell:

1) Prepare: Know your Vision, Outcome and Purpose
2) As long as you decide it will take
3) As many pages as it takes to say what you want to say

In my experience, I have seen that for some people, the idea of writing a book is as formidable a task as climbing a mountain! And the first thing I usually hear is "I would LOVE to write a book, but I don't know how or where to begin!"

Whether writing a book is a must for your business, something you think you would like to do, or a lifelong dream you have been yearning to fulfill, my promise is to demonstrate how you can get the book out of your head and onto the paper using a series of simple, foolproof techniques. The truth is, you CAN create your own book. How? By knowing what to do first. ***This book is about what to do first.***

For others, it's not how to start or the process itself that is so daunting, but the time required to complete it. After all, who has time to sit down and write a book? I've asked hundreds of people, "How long do you think it takes to write a book?" The typical answer is anywhere from 3 months to a year. I then ask, "How long do you think it would take YOU to write YOUR book?" These responses are very different and also vary enormously, from "I don't know, six months," to "two years" to "a decade!"

Writing a book takes as long as you decide it is going to take. And there are no minimum number of pages, either – a book needs only as many pages as it takes to say what you want to say.

People are always surprised to learn that writing a book doesn't have to take a long time and amazed when I tell them that they can complete their first manuscript in just a few weeks. *This book is about getting your book out of your head and onto the paper – quickly.*

I am going to show you how you can create your book in a short time by getting off to a great start. Your book will become a reality:

- As soon as you truly decide to take the first step
- When you are prepared to write
- When you know your vision, outcome and purpose for your book

This book will provide you with a framework for building your book's structure, creating content and completing a really great first draft of your book. I will also show you how to edit your book.

Using this Book

Writing a book probably seems like an arduous project and most people believe they need to set aside a big block of time. The truth is, you can write your book in just 30 to 45 minutes a day, *but more on that later!*

Keep this book handy. Read it and do the exercises, even if for only 10 minutes a day. It will get the juices flowing and start the ideas popping like Orville Redenbacher's kernels. I've purposely provided lots of space for you to write down ideas throughout the book as well as blank pages at the end.

In particular, complete the "Vision, Outcome, Purpose" in Chapter 2 and the "Describe Your Book" exercise in Chapter 8. Print them on colored paper and put them where you can see and read them every day. By the time you complete this workbook, not only will you know exactly how you are going to write your book, but *you will also be prepared and ready to write your book, this is my promise.*

If you are in a hurry and want to get started on your book as soon as possible, follow the "Get Started Today" instructions on the next page. You can be ready to begin your book in less than 10 days!

To your writing success!
Ann McIndoo

Get Started Today!

Instructions for Preparing to Write Your Book In 7 Days or Less!

Step 1: <u>**Set aside 30 minutes to devote to preparing to write your book**</u>

a. Choose a time that you can read this book and think about Your book
b. Select a location where you can fully engage and not be distracted
c. Have a pen you like to write with handy

Step 2: <u>**Read Chapters 1 and 2 of "So, You Want to Write!"**</u>

a. Complete the Writer's Identity Exercise
b. Complete the Vision Outcome Purpose Exercises
c. Complete the Writing Goals Exercise

You are on your way! Completing these exercises will give you clarity about your book, its mission and purpose. Knowing this makes it easier to keep moving forward when you hit a bump on your writing journey.

Step 3: <u>**Schedule 4 Writing Appointments**</u>

a. Mark your calendar "Writing Appointment with My Book"
b. Choose 4 days in the next week (or whatever time frame works for you)
c. Schedule 4 appointments: 30-45 minutes for each appointment
d. KEEP YOUR APPOINTMENTS!! Remember, no appointments = no book!
e. Use the sample Writer's Calendar in Chapter 4 to mark your writing appointments and make notes.

Step 4: Keep Your Writing Appointments!

Appointment #1: Read Chapter 3 through Chapter 5: Create Your Writer's Power Tools. Begin using them to prepare to write.

Appointment #2: Read Chapter 6 and Chapter 7: Start collecting all your notes and materials for your book.

Appointment #3: Read Chapter 8: Do the Speedwriting and Describe Your Book exercises – this is important! Read all of the book-writing strategies and select the one(s) that will work for you.

Appointment #4: Read Chapter 9 and Chapter 10: Create your Manuscript Grid™, Storyboard and Schedule Your Success!

You are on your way! To Your Writing Success!!!

The best way to become acquainted with a subject
is to write a book about it.

Benjamin Disraeli, (1804-81) Prime Minister of England and novelist

Finally holding my finished first book in my
hand was one of the most completely fulfilling moments of my life.
To think that it all started with just one idea.

Glenn Plaskin, author

Professionals! Become an Author in 2008!

Discover the Author in You and Write Your Book!

★ Being a Published Author gives You Credibility in Your Business

★ Become Known as the Expert in your Industry

★ Create a Platform for Ancillary Products & Generate Additional Revenue

★ Receive More Speaking Invitations ★ Earn Higher Speaking Fees

★ Learn how to Make Money with Your Book!

Author's Boot Camp for Professionals

Los Angeles * New York * Paris

Check www.AuthorsBootCamp.com for additional Locations and Dates

Have you always wanted to write your book but didn't know where to start? The tools and your Author's Coach are here, ready to help you write your book – **NOW!** I will show you how to transform a book idea in your head into a manuscript in your hands. Beginning with 6 private coaching sessions, I will help you create the structure for your book, organize your material and together, **create your book in as little as 8 weeks!** *I will also teach you how you can have your book published and create ancillary products so you can generate $$$ with your material.* Go to www.AuthorsBootCamp.com for full details and to register online or call for information.

So, You Want to Write!

www.SoYouWantToWrite.com ★ (760) 771-8940 ★ Ann@SoYouWantToWrite.com

Chapter 1

PREPARING FOR YOUR WRITING JOURNEY

"Between nothing and greatness are a lot of little steps"
Judy Osuna, Religious Science Practitioner

Welcome

Welcome! So, you want to write a book? Congratulations on your decision to write! The writing process can be a memorable experience and open many unexpected doors. I love writing. There is nothing like receiving a note of thanks or a phone call for helping someone because of something you wrote. For me, the sense of accomplishment and satisfaction is unmatched.

Who can write a book? Anyone! If you are an authority on a subject, possess a skill that others wish to learn or have specialized knowledge, are consumed with a burning desire to tell a story or teach others, **YOU** can write a book!

I'm curious. Have you been thinking about writing a book but didn't know how to get started? Did your not knowing how to organize your material, create an outline or use a storyboard stop you? Have you ever wondered how long it takes to write a book and what you would have to do to prepare? Have you started writing your book but have become stuck, slowed down by procrastination or not sure about your next step?

If you answered yes to any of these questions, you have come to the right place. I am going to answer all these questions and teach you how to write your book. Using examples and exercises, in the chapters that follow, you will learn:

★ How to prepare yourself to write – what to do BEFORE you pick up your pen (or sit at your laptop!)

★ How to get all of your content out of your head and onto the paper!

★ What to do with your research and notes – How to organize your material

★ How to stay motivated, deal with procrastination and "writer's block"

★ How to use writing technologies – simple, effective ways to produce content–quickly!

★ How to "Schedule Your Success™" You decide how soon you want to finish your book: 4, 6, or 8 weeks – in 1 hour a day.

★ How to edit your manuscript – simple steps to make this process easy.

Learning to write is like any other skill, *you get better with practice*. On your first visit to the gym, a trainer taught you how to use the equipment. On your next visit, you did a little more. As you continued working out, you increased your skill and stamina and begin seeing great results.

It is the same thing with writing. ***You learn to write by writing***. At first you may write just a few paragraphs or for just a few minutes. As time passes, you will notice that you will write more and for longer periods of time. You will soon see that it becomes much easier and can be most enjoyable.

What You Are Going to Learn

This book is about *preparation, organization, motivation and scheduled success*. You will learn about preparing yourself to write, organizing your material to create a book, staying motivated throughout the writing process and scheduling your success – i.e., *completing your book*. I will address these issues head-on as they are the issues that most writers face. I'm going to break them down into little bite-size chunks so it's easy and fun.

I am also going to teach you five simple, yet very effective, writing strategies that will get the content out of your head and onto the paper:

- ★ Speedwriting
- ★ Describe Your Book
- ★ Manuscript Grid
- ★ Storyboard
- ★ Chapter Questions

These are strategies I've used in the last 10 years working alongside many of the nation's leading motivational thinkers, self-help practitioners and self-made businessmen. I have seen what it takes to create extraordinary work and I am going to share these strategies with you in this book.

Finding Your Creative Zone

I would also like take you to a very special place – a place I call the "creative zone". On the next page, you will learn how to get to that amazing place where you become your most creative, that state of mind where you can't wait to write. You feel as if ideas are pouring into you and the words are just bursting out! You can't write fast enough! I think you will agree that you produce your best when you are excited and inspired about what you are doing.

Would you like to go there? Would you like to learn how you can get there anytime you want? Are you committed to finding your "creative zone"? Perfect! I will show you how you can find your "creative zone" and enter it anytime you wish in just a few simple steps.

Right now I want you to decide to make this a truly amazing experience and discover the author inside you!

Ready? **Let's go to the Creative Zone!**

Chapter 2

PREPARING:
WHAT TO DO **BEFORE** YOU PICK UP YOUR PEN!!

Getting into the Creative Zone

The first thing you want to do **_before you begin writing_** is to get into the creative zone – that magical place where everything comes out exactly the way
you want it. How do you know what your creative zone is? How do you know
when you are in it? What does it look like and how does it feel?

I've asked many writers, authors and speakers what their creative zones were
like and how they got there. It is different for everyone. The one thing that I
found was true for everyone was that _when they started to speak about it,_ **_they_**
got into it.

That "special place" is a magical place for sure, where you are totally "into"
what you are doing, like relishing a fine meal, enjoying passionate sex or los-
ing yourself in a fantastic movie. In this heightened, creative state, you are
totally concentrated and focused and your energy is pulsing through you. This
is "the zone" where all creativity flourishes.

When I'm in my creative zone, I feel:

- ★ Happy and excited – I can't wait to get started!
- ★ Unstoppable! I'm going to write everything I want!
- ★ Inspired – overflowing with ideas!
- ★ No sense of time – it just flies by!
- ★ Juicy – I have lots of content, ready to come out!

When I get into my creative zone, I cannot write fast enough! I start laughing and smiling and wow! What a great place to be. I enjoy and savor every minute.

The amazing part of this is that you can enter your creative zone *anytime you wish! As often as you like! For as long as you want!* I know this to be true, because I do it myself every day, using my Writer's Power Tools™.

In this chapter, I am going to prepare you to write with a brief overview of what I call my "Writer's Power Tools™". We will then create your writer's identity, determine your Outcome and Purpose for your book and write down your Top 10 Writing Goals, 3 Outrageous Goals and, of course, your Mother Lode Goal.

After this has been accomplished, you will be ready to create your own Writer's Power Tools™ which is the key that opens the door to your creative zone.

Overview of Writer's Power Tools

How do you get the juices flowing and start writing your book? **It all comes down to properly preparing to write.** The easiest and quickest way to get to your creative zone is to *be prepared* to write – on three levels:

1) Your head (what you say to yourself about writing)
2) Your body (how you feel about writing)
3) Your environment (where you write)

Here is a brief overview, so you know exactly what I mean. You'll be creating your own Writer's Power Tools™ in the next chapter.

Your Head: What do you say to yourself when you think about writing your "book"? What words describe your feelings about your book? What does this book mean to you? What gifts and "creative" power are you going to use to create your book? Whatever they are, *you want to wake them up!* Which **words** come to mind when you think about the amazing work that you are about to create? *Say them out loud.*

Your Body: Now, stand up and take on a strong sense of certainty. Stand strong, show confidence, feel the joy and gratitude about what you are going to do. Know in your heart and in your body that you are going to create something brilliant. Using this physiology, how does it feel when you think about your book?

What do you see? How do you walk, talk, breathe, when you think about yourself as a "writer"? Imagine and see the words, "best-selling Author" before your name. Put a great big smile on your face and say your name and "best-selling author" out loud. How does that feel?

Your Environment:

Pick your special "writing" place, a space to write. A place you can't wait to get to! It doesn't have to be fancy. It will be your "official" place to write. This is where you have your writing tools, journal, notes and research ready to use. My writing place is typically my office, but sometimes my writing place is a plastic lounge chair by the pool, a local Starbuck's or picnic table at the park.

I refer to these three levels of preparation as my "Writer's Power Tools™". I fire them up every day to get ready to write. We are going to create your Writer's Power Tools™ in Chapter 3; however, the very first step is to create and take on your *writer's identity*.

Creating Your Writer's Identity

Being prepared to write is absolutely critical. To start the process of preparing, one of the first things we are going to do is determine your *writer's identity*. You may be wondering what your identity has to do with writing. Well, think about this for a moment. Do you have children? If not, how about a favorite niece or nephew? Think about them for a minute. How do you feel? Do certain feelings come up for you? Perhaps you feel love, pride, accomplishment, satisfaction? When you have your "parent" identity on, how do you act? What role do you play? Leader? Nurturer? Caretaker?

How about in your professional life? When you think of a business professional, consultant, speaker, coach, doctor, or police officer, what identity comes to mind? What roles do they play? Now think of your own profession. What happens when someone asks you a question about your profession? You take on your professional identity. Everything you know about your profession comes to mind. You answer questions with certainty, and perhaps even offer advice.

It's the same thing with writing, whether it's fiction or non-fiction. When you have that same confidence and certainty about writing, you'll take on a writer's identity. ***The identity we assume and reinforce within ourselves will always become a reality.*** In other words, if you tell yourself you are an incisive, inspired writer, propelled by the power to help others, to communicate your message, so it shall be.

In the next few pages I'm going to ask you a series of questions to help you find your writer's identity. These questions will help you envision your book, imagine the writing possibilities, get your creative juices flowing and help you determine the *outcome and purpose* for your book. As I ask you the three series of questions, I want you to think about them, answer them in your head and *notice how it feels.*

Take your time, read them slowly and think about each question. Remember, answer each question in your head. After you finish reading the questions, seeing the answers in your mind's eye and answering them in your head, you can write down your answers in the exercises that follow.

Question 1:
WHAT IS YOUR VISION FOR YOUR BOOK AND YOURSELF?

What is it that you want to write? Do you want to create something that will teach? Inspire? Motivate? Generate revenue? Perhaps an eBook that you sell on the internet or a book you publish yourself. Is this your masterpiece?

What does your book look like? Close your eyes and envision it! What does the cover look like? Is it softbound or hardbound? Perhaps it is a spiral work-book. What color is it? Can you see the title of your book on it? How does it feel to see it?

Imagine yourself signing your book and handing it to readers at a book signing, people who are anxious to read your book. See yourself speaking to large audiences about your book. Envision yourself holding workshops of your own and sharing your information.

See yourself as a writer. See yourself as an author. How does that feel?   ·

When you think about writing, what is your identity? Below is a list of titles. Say each one aloud. As you say them, I want you to say your name before and after each one. Say them slowly. Notice how each one feels. Notice which ones you like, which ones feel really good, which ones compel you, attract you towards them.

For example, I'm going to say, "Writer." Ann McIndoo, Writer. Or, Writer, Ann McIndoo. With each one of these titles, say your name. Ready? Okay, here we go:

🖊 Writer   🖊 Author   🖊 Speaker
🖊 Coach   🖊 Consultant   🖊 Presenter

Which ones got you excited? Do any of them make you feel creative? What does it feel like to have these words after your name? Say them out loud. Say your name and the title you like the best. Repeat it, and this time get really excited about it. Smile when you say it, feel it, breathe it! Enjoy it! Celebrate it! How does that feel? Let's try a couple more:

- 🖊 Author and Speaker
- 🖊 Best-Selling Author
- 🖊 International Best-Selling Author
- 🖊 #1 International Best-Selling Author!
- 🖊 Radio and Television Personality

Exercise: CREATING YOUR WRITER'S IDENTITY

Which one is your favorite? Write your name and the title you chose in the box below. Write it a few times. How does it look? How does it feel? Try writing 2 or 3 different titles and see which one you like the best.

Once you select the one you like best, write it down with different color pens and pencils. Write it slow and elegant, then fast and excited. Finally, write it like you are endorsing your big fat advance check and how you will sign your name when you autograph books!

_____

_____

_____

_____

_____

_____

_____

_____

This is how I will autograph my books:

_____

_____

_____

_____

_____

Wasn't that fun? If you are thinking, "What does this have to do with writing?" just hang in there for a little bit. It will make sense soon and you will see what a powerful writing tool you are creating.

Question 2:
HOW SERIOUS AND COMMITTED ARE YOU TO WRITING YOUR BOOK?

Why do you want to write a book? Writing takes discipline, determination and dedication. Some might even say it is hard work.

I have found writing to be like wooing a lover – a teasing, exciting, passionate adventure. I always want more and can't wait for our next time together. I think of writing as a love affair with words. You fall in love with the words and the joy you get when, like a string of pearls, you put them together just right!

What does this book mean to you? Is this simply a hobby or is this a major creative force pulling you towards it? Are you willing to get up early to write, or stay up until the wee hours of the night dictating, scribbling, capturing ideas and jotting notes? Is this something you can't stop thinking about?

How do you feel about your own writing? What **words** come to mind when you think about writing your book? What **feelings** come up when you think about writing your book?

What steps are you willing to take to write your book?

What actions are you prepared to implement to write your book?

When you think about and answer these questions – how does it feel? Are you excited about getting started? Do you feel like an aspiring writer or an author ready to take on the challenge of an exciting new project?

Enjoy it and capture it in your memory and body – *remember what it feels like.*

Question 3:
HOW ARE YOU GOING TO PREPARE YOURSELF TO WRITE?

Preparing to write is about three things – engaging your mind, body and environment.

(1)   **Your Mind**: Getting your head in the right place, thinking about what you are going to write, knowing what you want to say, knowing your outcome. Thinking like a writer.

(2)   **Your Body**: Deciding, committing and resolving – in your mind and body to create your book. Your frame of mind, your "state" will determine how and what you are going to produce. *Your state will determine what you write.*

(3)   **Your Environment**: What is your writing environment? Is it ready and waiting? What tools will you be using?

What are you going to do to get ready to write your book?

How are you going to prepare?

Now that you have thought about these questions, answer them on the following pages.

Question #1: What is your vision for your book?

_____

_____

_____

_____

_____

_____

_____

_____

_____

_____

_____

_____

_____

_____

_____

_____

_____

_____

_____

_____

_____

_____

Question #2:
How serious and committed are you to writing and making your vision for your book come alive? What are you willing to do to make this happen? How much time are you willing to spend each day? 5 minutes? 10, 20, 45 minutes? How many days a week? 1, 2, 3, 5 days a week? Decide and commit.

Question #3:
What are you going to do to prepare? What action are you going to take that will get you closer to writing your book?

_____

_____

_____

_____

_____

_____

_____

_____

_____

_____

_____

_____

_____

_____

_____

_____

_____

_____

_____

Your Outcome and Purpose

Now we come to the **two most important questions that you must answer** before you can even begin to think about writing your book. They are:

*(1) What is your **Outcome** for this book?*
*(2) What is your **Purpose** for writing it?*

What is the importance of having an Outcome and Purpose? ***Everything!!!*** Without an outcome and purpose, there is no motive, no compelling future, no leverage for you to complete your book! Although they may seem similar, there is a distinct difference between Outcome and Purpose.

Outcome is the WHAT
> **What do you want to do with this book?**
> *What results do you want?*

Purpose is the WHY
> **Why must this book be written?**
> *Why do you want to write this book?*

Outcome

The first question is: ***What is your outcome for your book?*** What do you want to see happen with this book? What is this going to give you? Who are you going to become because of this? How will this make a difference in your life? In someone else's life? How will this impact your business or your financial status?

What does this book mean to you? What will this experience bring you? When you think about the possibilities of a book – what do you see? Can you visualize the title to your book in great big letters with your name underneath it? Can you see your book on Amazon.com? Can you see your books in a bookstore? Stacks of your book at Barnes & Noble? People reading it while sipping their coffee at Borders?

When you dream about this book, what is your outcome?

A friend of mine, Bobby Ruiz, competed in the Iron Man Triathlon in Kona, Hawaii. This is the big one, the race every tri-athlete dreams of. Qualifying for this race is one of the most rigorous in the world. Completing this race is a huge accomplishment. What made Bobby's experience so extraordinary, was that he prepared for the Iron Man Triathlon in *five months*! It usually takes two to three **YEARS** to train for a race like this.

Bobby is currently writing his book, *Zero to Iron Man in 5 Months* (www.ZeroToIronman.com) and his outcome is to inspire kids. This is what he says: "I don't care if anybody **ever** buys my book. I want to write my story and have a hardbound book that I can give to the kids when I speak at high schools." That's his outcome. To inspire and motivate kids to follow their dreams.

What is your outcome? What is your vision of your book? What do you want to accomplish with your book?

Purpose

The second question is: ***What is your purpose?*** Why must this book be written? Why do you want to write this book? What is your motive for writing? Do you want to tell your story or perhaps someone else's story? Do you want to inform? Teach? Motivate? Inspire? Is this a business tool or back of room product? What is your purpose for writing this book? It is a very, very important question.

A motivational speaker I have known for many years recently asked if I could help him write his first book. I asked him, why do you want a book? He said he was traveling all over the United States speaking and he wanted to be able to provide his material to the audience in the form of a book he could sell at the back of the rooms where he spoke. He wanted to make more money! That was his purpose – to earn more money.

A dear friend of mine, Jan Walker, who is a nurse, wrote a wonderful book called *Kids to the Rescue* (www.KidsToTheRescue.com). She wrote this book to teach children all about safety. Her *outcome* was to teach kids about safety, her *purpose* was to see fewer kids in the emergency room.

Answering these questions will give you **your outcome and purpose for writing**. When you have your outcome and your purpose clearly defined, you have a compelling reason to write and the motivation to prepare yourself, in your head, in your body and in your environment. And what happens when you are prepared to write? *You Write!*

So let's find out what your purpose and outcome are. Think about your answers to the questions above and write your Outcome and Purpose on the following pages.

The Outcome I want for my book is:

_____

_____

_____

_____

_____

_____

_____

_____

_____

_____

_____

_____

_____

_____

_____

_____

_____

_____

_____

_____

_____

_____

The Purpose for my book is:

_____

_____

_____

_____

_____

_____

_____

_____

_____

_____

_____

_____

_____

_____

Read your Outcome and Purpose often. Use it to inspire and motivate you. See yourself achieving your outcome. See your purpose being fulfilled. Ask yourself frequently: What steps can I take NOW to achieving my Outcome? What can I do today to fulfilling my Purpose? And then, take action! Take one step that will get you closer to your Outcome and Purpose.

Your Writing Goals

Now that you have determined what and why, let's talk about when. What are your Writing Goals? What are some of the goals you would like to achieve with your writing? On the next page, write down your top ten writing goals. Then on the following page, write your three most outrageous writing goals. Be playful – no limits! Then write down your "Mother Lode" goal. This is something Mark Victor Hansen, co-author of the *Chicken Soup for the Soul* series, teaches. It is a great way to think big, plan big, play big. Step up and get in the game! Here are some examples. Use them to inspire your own.

Writing Goals:

- ★ Decide on the name of my book by _____
- ★ Come up with the 10 major subjects in my book by _____
- ★ Create a Manuscript Grid™ for my book by _____
- ★ Create a storyboard for my book by _____
- ★ Complete my storyboard for my book by _____
- ★ Name the chapters of my book by _____
- ★ Complete a chapter every _____
- ★ Complete my book by _____
- ★ Complete my research by _____
- ★ Design the cover of my book by _____
- ★ Decide my publishing strategy by _____
- ★ Complete the editing on my book by _____

Outrageous Goals:

- ★ Publish my book in the next _____ days
- ★ Create a seminar or workshop based on my book
- ★ Generate $_____ in revenue from my book at speaking events
- ★ Create ancillary products and sell them online
- ★ Do a National Book tour
- ★ See my book make #1 Best Seller on Amazon.com
- ★ Be on the *New York Times* Best Seller list
- ★ See my book sell like hot cakes at Barnes & Noble

Mother Lode Goals

- ★ Be a guest on Oprah!
- ★ See my book translated into 5 languages!
- ★ See my book become an international best seller!

<u>My Top Ten Writing Goals</u>

	GOAL #	GOAL AND COMPLETION DATE
1		
2		
3		
4		
5		
6		
7		
8		
9		
10		

Three Outrageous Writing Goals

Now write down your top three OUTRAGEOUS Writing Goals. I'm talking out-of-this-world, over-the-top. What would you like to accomplish that at this very moment seems amazing, astonishing, astounding, remarkable, wonderful, incredible, marvelous, miraculous, mind-blowing and totally outrageous?

GOAL #	GOAL AND COMPLETION DATE
1	
2	
3	

<u>My Mother Lode Writing Goal</u>

My Mother Lode goal is by _____, I will

When you have completed writing your Mother Lode goal, take a few minutes and get up and walk around a bit. Then come back and read your Mother Lode goal again. See yourself achieving your goal. Visualize yourself enjoying your accomplishments.

How does it make you feel? Do you get excited thinking about your future? Does reading this goal get you excited and anxious to get started? Yes? Outstanding! If a little fear shows up, that's okay! That just means you are thinking beyond your comfort zone, that you are going to learn and grow! Remember, fear simply means we are going to stretch ourselves and learn something new.

Now, make five copies of your Mother Lode Goal on colored paper. Place them on your desk or wall so you can read it every day while you are working, on your nightstand so you can see it when you wake up and before you go to sleep, in a kitchen drawer, in your car, and in your briefcase – where you can see it and read it several times a day.

Each time you read your Mother Lode Goal,
visualize yourself achieving it and see yourself doing it,
imagine how it feels.

Think of what resources you can use to get you closer to your
goal, what steps you can take NOW to make your
Mother Lode Goal become a reality.

> ★ **Keep a small notebook handy**
> ★ **Write down all the ideas you get**
> ★ **TAKE ACTION!**

With your new Writer's Identity, you are now a Writer!
Do 1 thing each day that will get you closer to your goal.

I am currently working with an author who sets his "Opportunity Clock" at 5:30 am each morning, which is a half-hour earlier than usual. He uses these 30 minutes each day to work on his book. In a recent coaching call, he mentioned that since he had started doing this, he was amazed at the progress he had made. In just 30 minutes a day! What time will your opportunity clock go off?

Chapter 3

CREATING YOUR WRITER'S POWER TOOLS

Writers: Start Your Engines!

Now that you have learned about preparing to write, know your writer's identity, have your book's outcome and purpose in mind, you have your writing goals ready and waiting, you are ready to create your Writer's Power Tools™!

What are the Writer's Power Tools and why do I need them? Happy you asked!

Your Writer's Power Tools™ are your:

(1) **Power Script: What you say to yourself as you prepare to write**
(2) **Power Move: How you prepare your body**
(3) **Power Anchors: Your environment and tools**

Your Writer's Power Tools™ will get you into your creative state.
They will generate inspiration, positive attitude
and the expectation of success.

Examples of Writer's Power Tools™

A friend of mine, who writes for a large family magazine, has a unique Power Script, Power Move and Power Anchors. His writing appointment is from 8:30 am until 1:00 pm every day. Come heck or high water, that's when he writes. If he doesn't feel well or not in the mood, he says to himself, "Get your lazy a—out of bed. Go write." And he does. That's his Power Script, "Get your a—out of bed."

He also has his "writing" environment. He sits at his desk and computer and wears a white T-shirt, a pair of khaki shorts, no shoes and white socks. The shorts are his lucky "writing" shorts. He doesn't write without them!

He has a very distinct way of sitting. When he's ready to write, he crosses his legs and sits up. His eyes look up while he thinks and then he puts his hands on the keyboard, like a pianist, briefly closes his eyes and then starts typing and the magic comes through. This is how he writes. ***These are his writing scripts.***

Another writer I know will stop for a minute before typing and think about things. She will close her eyes and start rubbing her temples. She thinks about what she wants to say. It is almost like she is massaging her brain, waking it up. All of sudden, her eyes will pop open, one leg starts tapping and I know she is in her creative zone. She will dictate fifteen, twenty, thirty minutes of brilliant content. ***These are her writing scripts.***

Think of something that you are really great at doing, e.g., cooking, playing golf, sewing, a hobby or sport. What do you do before you start? You make plans, put on certain clothes, go to a certain place, gather your tools or equipment or buy supplies and think about how much fun you are going to have. _This is your script for this particular activity._

One final example that I'd like to share with you is what I do to prepare to write. I like to prepare as I walk to my writing place or once I arrive there – definitely before I sit down!

My Power Script

My belief is that my creativity begins in my head. I imagine the words dancing over my head, my creative thoughts and ideas in a colorful rainbow. I visualize them coming from my head through my heart, so they are touched with joy and love. Then I send them through my arms, out to my hands and fingers where they land on the keyboard and appear on my computer screen.

While I'm visualizing all the extraordinary work I plan to do, with my eyes closed, I say: "Yes! Yes! Yes! I love to write! This is exactly what I want to do, I'm excited about writing. I can't wait to write. I am so, so lucky that I get to do this today".

When I am going to write with a client, I close my eyes and say the following words several times before we work together:

"I am dedicated to the outcome of this book. My purpose is to serve the greatest good. I'm here as a scribe knowing that I will not let outside influences change my focus and outcome. I have the magnificence within me to be in this arena. Between nothing and greatness, there are lots of little steps."

By the time my client arrives, I'm in a heightened state of anticipation – physically energized, motivated and ready to write. There's no other place I'd rather be. In short, I am in the creative zone we talked about. When you are in that zone, you are unstoppable! The next thing I do is make my power move.

My Power Move

I close my eyes and visualize all the amazing things I am going to create. I clap my hands four, five, six times really fast and loud. I rub them together and get them hot. I do this three times and I say, "Yes! Yes! Yes!" I repeat my Power Script: "I love this. This is so much fun." I keep clapping and rubbing. Smiling the whole time. "I'm feeling great, feeling excited, happy to have the opportunity to do this. Today I feel amazing and creative and will create extraordinary things".

Now I look at my visual power anchors.

My Power Anchors

At this point, I am in the zone, I am excited to write, and my body is vibrating with possibilities. I also have some favorite writing "gear". Like my friend, I have a favorite writing shirt that I like to wear. It's old and worn, but it has been with me around the world and it's soft and comfy and I have written many books in it.

Now I go and sit in one of my favorite writing places. My "official" writing spot is at my desk with my laptop. I have my magic "writing" pen handy and a spiral notebook I use to jot down ideas and action items. From my writing spot, I can look out and see grass and trees. I can open the doors leading to a patio and feel a breeze and hear birds chirping. Sometimes I light candles, or I play my favorite "writing" music. To me, it's a magical place. This is my magic writing spot.

I frequently go out on the patio with my favorite writing pen and a spiral notebook and write about what I want to write about. I also take my digital recorder* – *I never go anywhere without it!* When I find that I can't write my ideas down fast enough – I simply start recording my thoughts and ideas. That's one of the key benefits about having your writing spot – **it's a place to keep your writing tools handy**. When you find yourself in your creative zone, you don't want to interrupt it by looking for a pen and paper!

I have created a variety of writing places for myself and have a small writing memo pad and pen in every room in my home, yes, including the closet! You never know when you are going to get a great idea and you want to be able to just start writing! Sometimes, just seeing a pen and pad fires up my desire to write.

Remember, your environment doesn't have to be a fancy office. Just a great spot where you feel comfortable, where you have your writing tools handy and where you can focus on your writing.

A great way to determine when you have found your "spot" is to notice how you feel when you are there. Do you feel right? Do you feel ready, excited, creative? Then you've got your head and body in the right place. You're in an amazing environment. This is your magical place.

These are the steps I use to prepare to write. I truly love writing and have triggered off my Power Script, Power Move and Power Anchors so often that it's quite easy for me to prepare. It can be the same for you, it is just a matter of practice. You can do the same!

So, . . . do you have a:

  ✓ Power Script?
  ✓ Power Move?
  ✓ Power Anchors?

Yes, of course you do! You just don't realize what they are. Let's figure out what they are. Yes! Right now!

*Digital Recorder: I use an Olympus DM-20. It is an incredible piece of equipment – small, light, easy to use. It stores up to 45 hours of content – voice and music. You can copy your audio files to your computer for listening, transcribing and of course, backup! Another benefit is you can convert these audio files to MP3 format and create your own audio products. I have purchased several dozen (each author I work with gets one) and buy them from www.zipzoomfly.com.

Creating Your Power Script - Power Move - Power Anchors

Let's start with your Power Script. How can you figure out what your Writing Power Script is? Ask yourself questions about what you do before you write and how you write.

Power Script:

> *To come up with your Power Script, ask yourself the following questions:* What does writing mean to you? What gets you juicy? What do you say to yourself when you think about or plan to write? What do you say to get creative? What words describe your feelings about writing? About your book? What do you see when you think about your book? What are your ideas? What does this book mean to you? What gifts and "creative" power are you going to use? ***Wake them up!*** What **words** come to mind when you think about the amazing work that you are about to create? ***Write them down!*** *This is your Power Script.*

Think of the last time you had a really great writing session. What did you say to yourself before you began writing? Write down these words and the words you say when you are just about to write. Write down the words that come to mind when you answer the questions above. If none come to mind, what would you say to yourself to become inspired and excited about writing? Think of a time in your past that you were inspired and creative, what did you say to yourself at that time?

For example, my words and phrases are:

- ✓ Yes! Yes! Yes!
- ✓ I love to write!
- ✓ I am so lucky!
- ✓ This is what I want to do!

What are some of your power words? What words or phrases do you say to yourself to get inspired, excited or ready to take action? Think of the words that you want to include in your Power Script. Write them down below. *(If none come to mind, write a few that you find inspiring and would like to say).*

- ✓ _____
- ✓ _____
- ✓ _____

My Power Script is just a few short sentences that I say over and over:

"Yes! Yes! Yes! I love to write! This is exactly what I want to do. I am so excited about writing. I can't wait to write. I am so, so lucky that I get to do this today. Thank you, God, thank you, Universe, for this magnificent gift".

By the time I have said this three or four times out loud, my entire focus is on what I am going to write.

To create your Power Script, take the power words you wrote above and create a few short sentences or action phrases. *They don't have to be about writing. They only need to inspire you to create.*

My Power Script:

_____

_____

_____

_____

_____

_____

_____

_____

_____

_____

_____

_____

_____

_____

_____

_____

_____

_____

_____

_____

That was fun! Okay, let's create our Power Move. How can you figure out what your power move is?

Power Move:

> *To come up with your Power Move, ask yourself the following questions:* What physical movements do you make before or during the writing process?
>
> What actions do you take to get ready to write? What does your body tend to want to do? Walk around? Pace back and forth? Sit quietly? Do you close your eyes, center yourself to a peaceful state?
>
> How does it feel when you think about your book? What do you see? How do you walk, talk and breathe, when you think about yourself as a "writer"? Visualize the words, "best-selling author" before your name. Say it out loud. How does that feel? Say it again! Loud and strong, really believe it, really enjoy it. ***Write this down!*** Write down how it feels to be a best-selling author.

_____

_____

_____

_____

_____

_____

Another way to determine your Power Move is to **have someone watch you get to that great place, watch you write and then tell you what your power move is**. Ask them to notice your physical movements, the way you sit, breathe, look, the position of your head, eyes, hands – have them notice every detail of your physical movements. You may have to do this several times to get every nuance of what your power move is.

Again, think of the last time you had a really great writing session. How did you get ready physically? Just as we stretch before running, what do you do before writing? Write down the words or short phrases that best describe physical movements you make on the next page. For example, my words, movements and beliefs are:

★ Yes! Yes! Yes!
★ I love this!
★ Clapping my hands
★ Rubbing my hands together
★ Smiling and laughing
★ Believing in myself
★ Knowing that what I want to write will come through me

What movements do you make when you are excited, achieve a goal, or experience a win? What victory movements do you make? Write them down:

Remember my Power Move?

I close my eyes and visualize all the amazing things I am going to create. I clap my hands 4, 5, 6 times really fast and loud. I rub them together and get them hot. I do this three times and I say, "Yes! Yes! Yes!" I repeat my incantation: "I love this. This is so much fun." I keep clapping and rubbing, smiling the whole time. "I'm feeling great, feeling excited, happy to have the opportunity to do this. Today I feel amazing and creative and will create extraordinary things".

Are you ready? Now take some of the words and phrases from your Power Script and combine them with the physical movements you like to make when you celebrate or get a huge win.

Write down your Power Move. Start with what comes to mind immediately. As you begin to use it and repeat it over and over, your Power Move will evolve into something that becomes a very natural and very powerful tool.

My Power Move:

_____

_____

_____

_____

_____

_____

_____

_____

_____

_____

_____

_____

_____

_____

_____

_____

_____

_____

_____

_____

Power Anchors:

> *To come up with your Power Anchors, ask yourself the following questions:* Where do I feel comfortable writing? Would it be at a desk, in bed, at the kitchen table, out on the patio? One of my clients loves to write at Starbucks and I absolutely love writing on an airplane. What environment makes me feel comfortable? Where is my favorite spot where I can sit and time seems to pass without notice? Where can I feel relaxed, comfortable and able to focus?
>
> A place you enjoy being, an environment you can't wait to get to! Select a location and try in on for size. How does it feel? If it feels inviting and welcoming, decide for now that this is your writing place. Look at it, visualize yourself writing, creating, producing there. Make it your "spot". If the first location you select doesn't quite work, try another. You will know you have the right writing environment when you realize you are spending a lot of time writing in it! Keep adjusting until you get it just right! This is a key component to your writing success.
>
> Having your writing tools and writing "gear" is also essential. I have notebook for my notes and journal. I like using a certain pen to write and a couple of writing souvenirs that always remind me of a great writing session.

Think of the last time you had a really great writing session. Where were you? Write down short phrases that describe your perfect writing spot, things that remind you of a great writing experience. What words that come to mind when you answer the questions above?

For example, phrases that describe my environment and location:

- ★ Quiet and peaceful, a cup of hot tea, soft music with no words
- ★ My favorite writing pen: Blue Pilot Precise Deluxe Bold
- ★ My writing place: my desk, laptop at the ready
- ★ Wearing my writing shirt, bare feet

Now write some of yours:

_____

_____

_____

_____

_____

Some additional Power Anchors that I have around me when I prepare to write are items I have used in the past while writing, gifts given to me by my clients while we wrote together and little charms or souvenirs I have picked up on my writing trips.

For example:

★ My lucky writing shirt – this has been with me for many years and I always have a great writing session when I wear it.

★ A beautiful Mont Blanc pen that was given to me by Tony Robbins. I have it on my desk and use it during my writing sessions.

★ A set of 5 gold keys that I received at a conference. They have the following engraved on them: Vision, Choices, Possibilities, Dreams and Faith. I pick them up, give them a shake and set them down and see how they land. I think about each virtue and how it's going to serve me today.

★ My Author hat. It says "Author" on the front and "Ask Me About My Book" on the back. I've given one to each author when they finished their book and looking at it always puts a huge smile on my face.

★ A wooden heart hanging on a stand. It reminds me to keep my heart in my writing.

★ A paperweight given to me by my dear friend, Loren Slocum, author of *No Greater Love* and founder of Lobella (www.Lobella.com) It has a great quote by Winston Churchill: Never, Never, Never, Quit!

These are a few of my favorite Power Anchors. When I look at these "anchors" and think about where they came from or how I got them, they associate me to something great about writing. Perhaps an amazing writing session or a wonderful writing experience.

The "Never Never Never Quit" paperweight reminds me to keep moving forward, to make it even better. All of these items make it very easy for me to get into a writing frame of mind, to get excited about writing and truly enjoy the process.

When I travel, I always take two or three of my Power Anchors with me. I put them on the work desk or the night stand in my hotel room. They remind me that I can write anytime I want to. On longer trips, I literally transform my hotel room into a powerful writing place by setting it up with my favorite items, which include two stuffed teddy bears (Larry and Billy), family photos, candles, a colorful shawl and a couple of my desk items.

Now write down some of your Power Anchors. If you don't have any official Power Anchors yet, what items do you currently have around you that inspire you? What interesting or fun things could you add to your writing place to stimulate your creativity and desire to write?

My Power Anchors:

_____

_____

_____

_____

_____

_____

_____

_____

_____

_____

_____

_____

_____

_____

_____

_____

_____

You Are In the Zone!

You did it! You have now created your very own Writer's Power Tools™. Now let's test them and see if they work! Here's how:

1. Stand up, walk around and shake it off. Drink some water and clear your thoughts.

2. When you are ready to write, say your Power Script. Say it loud and clear, several times with certainty and excitement.

3. Make your Power Move. Do it several times until your body is ready and you are excited about the possibilities.

4. Go to your writing spot, look at your Power Anchors and savor the memory of the writing experiences that they bring to mind.

5. Sit down and begin writing!

This takes practice! At first you may need to trigger your Power Tools several times each before feeling ready.

To make these even more powerful, get yourself in your creative zone and once you recognize it – **write it down**! What did you do? How does your body feel? What does it look like? What position are you in? Where are you?

When you get in that magic place, start writing and have someone watch you and tell you what your scripts are: how you look, how you sit, how you breathe, everything about what you do. Write it down and repeat this process. This is your script for getting into your creative zone, your key to creating magic!

When you have a challenge getting prepared, you can use your Writer's Power Tools™ to easily get in the creative zone because *you know exactly what to do*. That's a key part to writing. **You are now prepared to write**.

Chapter 4

LET'S WRITE! SCHEDULE YOUR SUCCESS!

The Writing Appointment

What's the next step? To **Schedule Your Success!**, of course!

Now that you know how to prepare to write, *the next step is to take action and schedule it*. **Make writing appointments**. *Writing every day is a great way to improve your writing skills*. Writing is a skill and it requires practice. How often do you think Michael Jordan, Tiger Woods and Lance Armstrong practice?

You can purchase or make yourself a Writing Calendar and schedule your writing appointments. (I have provided a sample at the end of this chapter.) Write your appointments and keep them! Make it a daily ritual, a regular routine, even if you only write for 5 minutes. If you do not write on a consistent basis, you will forget where you are and lose interest, and when you do come back to it, it will take longer to get back to where you were.

There are two rules when making a writing appointment:

> *Rule #1: Make your writing appointment and keep it! and*

> *Rule #2: Set reasonable and obtainable goals.*

Rule #1: Make Your Writing Appointment and Keep it!

Pick a time and place to write. Know your outcome for the appointment. How are you going to spend your time? What are the results you are expecting from this writing appointment?

Make sure there are no distractions – telephone, television, etc. Your Writing Appointment is just like anything else that is really important to you. What would make you want to keep any appointment? A compelling future! So make your appointments compelling! Tell yourself:

→ It's time to write! Everything I want to write is ready to be written, I can't wait to sit down and write today!

→ I am going to make a difference with this book. This weekend is the perfect time for me to write, plus I get to spend time doing something I love!

→ I'm going to write the most amazing things on Monday between 8:30 am and 10:30 am. *(Of course, don't limit yourself to these hours – choose your own!)*

→ I'm going to work on my book on Tuesday afternoon for 1 hour and complete the introduction to Chapter 1.

Make your writing appointment and keep it.

This is critical: *Keep your appointment to write.* **No appointments = no book**. Think about it. How does that feel? Ugh! Give your writing the same priority as the most important appointment with *your future*. Think about it, get excited about it, look forward to it and do it! *This is an appointment with your destiny.* Keep your writing appointments!

If you are new to writing, try different times of the day or evening. After a few writing sessions, you will see what time works best for you. Some writers I know like to write in the morning; a few of my author friends like to write in the afternoon. It's all up to you and your schedule. I typically start at 6:30 a.m. and schedule two hours. Sometimes I look up and find that it's already 10:00 am and I'm still in the flow and don't want to stop! But I do. I make myself stop, even though I'm still juicy and want to keep on writing.

Here's why. You want to keep the enthusiasm up and the momentum going. This is a writing strategy that I have found to be very helpful to keep my writing momentum going.

I rarely look at the clock. I just start writing and keep writing until I am almost done. That is when I stop writing. **<u>I never wait until I am tired of writing.</u>** *I stop before that point so I leave my writing appointment while I have momentum, while I am excited and in a great writing state.*

This writing strategy makes it exciting and compelling for me to come back to my next writing session. I can't wait to start my next appointment because I know I will be able to get to that same great place very quickly and continue writing.

Try this for a few days and see what happens.

I consider the "writing appointment" strictly for writing or brainstorming (about what I am writing), "creative thinking" time. Nothing else. Gathering notes and research is part of my "prep" time.

As I said, my scheduled writing time is 6:30 am - 8:30 am. I spend another 30 minutes or hour sometime during the day doing prep or research work. The last thing I do at night is clear my desk and get ready for my writing appointment the next morning. I take all business and "to do" items off my desk and set up my writing materials along with my Storyboard, book pages, pen and pad – all ready to go.

Your writing appointment can be anything you want it to be. Journaling, writing, research, just thinking about what you want to write. It's **your** appointment!

Writing Rituals

Many of the writers I know have a writing "ritual". They do certain things in a certain order to prepare to write. Here's my writing ritual:

It starts the night before I write. I do two things:

1. I decide when and where I am going to write the next morning. Since it is typically first thing in the morning at my desk, I clear off all business and miscellaneous items and put out my Writer's Kit, book materials and supplies I will be using.

2. Before I go to sleep, I smile and think about my writing appointment the next morning. I look forward to it and know that it will be a great session. I ask myself questions about my topic and what I want to write about. I start each question with: "What would be the best way to write . . . to describe . . . to inspire . . .".

I wake up at 6 and do my morning ritual -- feed my pup, open the windows, and make some tea, etc., all the while triggering my power tools: saying my Power Script, making my Move, anticipating going to my writing place as if I'm waiting to go on a date!

When I get to my desk, I put on some of my favorite music, maybe light a candle and hang my "Author" hat on my door. This is a signal to anyone coming near my office that I am in session and unavailable. Unless the house is on fire – Do Not Disturb!!!

When I sit down at my desk, I am excited to be there, looking forward to writing and nothing gets in my way! Can you imagine being excited at 6:30 am? It is an amazing feeling that lasts the entire time I am writing. I do it every writing day and I absolutely love it!

Water or bathroom breaks are the only reasons I get up during my writing appointment. I do not answer the phone or go online. While most writers consider research part of their writing time, I do not. I feel "unfaithful" if I am not writing, thinking about writing or reading my writing during my writing appointment, but that is my own rule. I have found that this strict guideline allows me to make very fast progress on a project. If I go online to do research, it is after my appointment, otherwise, it's too tempting to check e-mail because then all is definitely lost!

When you start to write, begin right where you left off. DO NOT READ YOUR MATERIAL FROM THE BEGINNING! If you start reading from the beginning, there is no doubt you will get involved in the editing process. Leave that alone – you can edit later. Right now it is time to write, to create new content. I usually read the last few paragraphs of what I wrote in my last writing session and then begin writing new content.

Everyone has their own rituals, whether it's lighting candles, music, deep breathing, a special pair of "writing shorts". Whatever gets you centered and focused are the tools you can use to create your own ritual.

To get you started in creating your own ritual, name or list some of the things you might do or have around you:

_____

_____

_____

_____

Rule #2: Set Inspiring and Realistic Goals

When making your appointment, set inspiring and realistic goals:

→ I'm going to write five pages

→ I am going to come up with three chapter titles

→ I am going to write for one hour and finish the first half of Chapter 1.

What are your expectations for completing your book? What would be a reasonable timeframe? What writing schedule could you set up that would be obtainable and sustainable? Set your writing goals and follow through.

If you are serious about writing, you must make time for it. This doesn't mean huge blocks of time, hours and hours. Depending on your writing goals, you can start with just 15 minutes a day. Here are some ideas:

🖉 Use a digital recorder and dictate your ideas or content *(I'll show you in Chapter 8 how you can "talk" your book in one weekend)*

🖉 Write on the subway to and from work, or on your lunch hour

🖉 Make notes and jot down interesting ideas and words while you are waiting in line at the bank or market, waiting for a pal at the lunch table

🖉 Get up one hour earlier and write

🖉 Instead of watching TV, surfing the net or talking on the telephone, write!

🖉 Going on a business trip? Perfect! You can write at the airport, while waiting for your flight on the airplane, or in your hotel room – wherever it is quiet and you are undisturbed

What days and times could you work on your book? Write down four times during the week when you can take 15 minutes to write and work on your book:

1. _____
2. _____
3. _____
4. _____

Your Writer's Calendar

One way to keep your writing momentum going is to have a Writer's Calendar with scheduled writing appointments. Use the sample Writer's Calendar on the following page (which can be used for any month in the year) to create your own Writer's Calendar.

Schedule your Writing Appointments and use it to mark:

✓ Weekly Writing Goals and Outcomes

✓ Writing Goals for the Month

✓ Book Goals and Outcomes

✓ Completed Writing appointments

✓ Great writing sessions – put stars on those pages and write down what made that session so great. Where did you write? How were you feeling? What did you do to prepare before your session?

✓ Start time, length and outcome for your writing appointments

✓ Target dates: Chapter completion dates, creating content for new topic, naming the chapters, completing the research.

✓ Completion Dates: subjects, topics, chapters, the manuscript!

✓ Editing Schedule

So, You Want to Write! Writer's Calendar
FOR YOUR WRITING APPOINTMENTS

(1) Fill in the numbers for the days of the month you are working in
(2) Mark your Writing Appointments in colored pen
(3) Fill in your writing goals and outcome for the month
(4) Fill in great writing appointments and what made them special

	Sun	Mon	Tues	Wed	Thurs	Fri	Sat
Outcome for the Month							
Complete by end of Week #1							
Complete by end of Week #2							
Complete by end of Week #3							
Complete by end of Week #4							

You can download a free Writer's Calendar at www.SoYouWantToWrite.com, click on the Resources page, Writing Tools and select Writer's Calendar.

Chapter 5
WRITING WARM-UPS AND TOOLS

Your Tools of the Trade

Here are some tools and strategies that may make writing a little easer:

- → Journaling
- → Writer's Prompts
- → www.LifeJournal.com
- → Procrastination: What's Really Happening?
- → Three Keys to Defeating Procrastination
- → Writer's Action Steps to Keep Writing
- → How to Break Through the Writer's Block Barrier!

The Importance and Benefits of Journaling

"Thoughts will come, but hush them away. Hush your thoughts until you are empty and breathing. Don't despair if you don't do this easily. Don't think about how it is not working. Just hush and hush again. Make the exhalation very long. 'Hush-sh-sh-sh-sh-sh-sh-sh.'
-Eric Maisel in Deep Writing: 7 Principles That Bring Ideas to Life

Why journal? There are so many benefits to journaling that it's difficult to just pick one. Besides remembering an event or a magic moment, it is a great way to prepare. I journal every day, even if it is just for three or four minutes. Having a special pen, a specific journaling book or specific place is not a requirement, but it does add some magic.

Journaling is one of those wonderful gifts you can give yourself anywhere, anytime. I have journaled on napkins, paper towels, airline ticket jackets, and receipts. When traveling, I always journal a note about my experience on a postcard and send it to myself. What a treat to receive them when I get home! And – It's another great Power Anchor. I have all my travel post cards up on in a wall in my office. I can't help but smile and remember something great about the places I have traveled to.

Yes, you can always *prepare* to journal, but that is one of the magical gifts of journaling – *it prepares you!*
Here are some additional benefits to journaling:

1) Journaling is a great way to warm up. Journal for five to 10 minutes before your write. You will notice a shorter prep time.

2) Capture ideas. Write about something you want to write about. Let the ideas come to you and write them down!

3) Create something – a scene, a character, a technique, a strategy.

4) Release. Write about something inside you that you want to let go of. Journaling can be a cleansing. Write it and then destroy it.

When journaling, don't think, just write and do not edit. This should just come through you. Don't try to make it anything, just write. Assume that no one will ever read your journal and write honestly. If you find it difficult to write about something or are embarrassed, shred it when you are done. This will give you the confidence and freedom to journal about anything you wish.

Let's give journaling a try. Write about yourself or anything else you want, for five minutes. Here are a few suggestions you can write about:

✓ Your surroundings

✓ A magic moment you enjoyed recently

✓ How you feel about something going on in your life, your family, your children, your accomplishments

✓ Your plans and dreams for the future

Take five minutes and journal:

_____

_____

_____

_____

_____

_____

_____

_____

_____

_____

_____

_____

_____

_____

_____

_____

Using Writer's Prompts

Another great tool you can use to start writing is known as Writer's Prompts. These are nothing more than possible ideas and topics to write about.

Look at the list of Writer's Prompts below. In addition to a topic, they typically give you a writing assignment. Pick one of the following prompts and write about it for five minutes. Just write – don't "think" about anything. You will be amazed at what comes out!

WRITER'S PROMPTS

1. You discover your pet can talk! What would you say to it? What do you think it would tell you?

2. What is one of the most magical moments in your life?

3. You have been given a magical power – what is it and how will you use it?

4. Travel in time – where would you go? Would you change anything?

5. You discover you can fly, but only at night. Where would you go? What would you do?

6. Describe your very best birthday!

7. What are you going to do with the proceeds of your #1 best seller!

Let's try journaling again. This time, use one of the prompts above and write for five minutes.

_____

_____

_____

_____

_____

Did you find the Writer's Prompts helpful? I noticed that I used prompts quite a bit when I first started writing. Over time, as I wrote more often, I didn't need the prompts as much and eventually, I created my own prompts.

If you enjoyed the prompts above and would like a few more, you can download as many as you like from my website, www.SoYouWantToWrite.com. Look on the Resources Page under "Free Downloads."

Would you like to learn more about a great journaling tool? Go to my site, www.SoYouWantToWrite.com.and click on the Resource page, then click on www.LifeJournal.com. This is wonderful software program that provides prompts and strategies for journaling. It is an excellent way to practice writing.

I like to journal for a few minutes before my writing appointment. Journaling is fun, it conjures up the creative juices, and gives you an opportunity to get stuff off your mind. It can also provide you with new material that can be used later.

Every few weeks, go back and review your journals. Note the date, amount of time you are writing and what kind of writing you are doing. This will indicate the direction of your interests. Use stars or dots to set deadlines, mark victories, remember great writing sessions.

What to Do When Fear (AKA Procrastination) Shows Up

What happens when it's time for your writing appointment and life shows up? The kids need you to drive them to soccer practice, you're tired or busy with work, or, the most scariest of all, you *are not in the mood*? Now what?

Your vision, level of commitment, driving force and belief of your book's compelling future will determine your writing mood. "Not being in the mood" is simply an emotion. *Not being in the mood or coming up with an excuse is simply fear.* We're not talking about *time*, we're talking about your *attitude*. What's going on in your head? What inner game are you playing? What meaning have you attached to writing?

Are you telling yourself a story? What are you saying to yourself? I have another question for you. Be honest. In this same "*not in the mood*" frame of mind, would you be willing to walk to your mailbox to retrieve $10,000 cash? If you perked up and said Yes!, but at the thought of keeping your writing appointment, your shoulders sagged, then we need a little preparation! *This is an appointment with your destiny. This is an appointment with your future. You don't want to miss it! No excuses!*

So, what are you going to do when fear shows up? What are you going to do when you are "not in the mood"? Are you going to come up with an excuse? Are you going to be a "no show" for your writing appointment?

Sometimes, when fear comes up, we start asking ourselves dumb questions. What if I write something stupid? What if nobody likes it? What if it doesn't sell? You know what? Forget about that. Don't worry about getting it perfect. The first step is getting it on paper – there will be plenty of time to edit later. That's what professional editors are for and love to do!

> **When fear, anxiety, stress, nervousness –**
> **the enemies of creativity, vision, imagination and resourcefulness –**
> **show up:**
>
> ✓ **Change what's going on in your head,**
> ✓ **Shake your body out**
> ✓ **Change your environment.**

How can you change:

→ **What's going on in your head?**
→ **How your body feels?**
→ **Your environment?**

You can do several things:

★ **To change what is going on in your head, ask yourself better questions:**

How am I going to approach writing differently today? What's really going on? One of my favorites is, Who's driving this bus? Me or fear? We already know that FEAR is False Evidence Appearing Real. What is this going to cost me if I don't do it? Why don't I want to sit down and write? What's really going on? Say to yourself, "The truth is . . . " and be honest! **Ask yourself better questions and answer them honestly**.

★ **To change how your body feels, get physical!**

Stand up and shake it off. Drink some water, take the dog for a walk, or go outside and get some air. Do a simple physical chore that requires no thought like taking out the trash, watering the grass or sweeping off the porch. This will give your body movement. Take this time to think about what you want to write about.

★　**To change your environment, take better actions:**

(1) **Commit to make every minute count for a specific amount of time**. Two to five isn't going to work out?　Work from 1:30 to 2:30 instead.　**Take a chunk, commit to that smaller chunk and do it**. Play full out and make every minute count in that shorter appointment. You can still take the kids to soccer, and when you come back, you are going to make those minutes count.

(2) **Review your outcome and purpose – what this means to you**. Read your Outcome and your Purpose for writing your book.　Sometimes just thinking about what it means to you and the reason you're doing it gets you back into that great writing place.

(3) **Read Your Goals**.　Grab your goal sheet, stand up and, if possible, go outside where you can get some fresh air.　Breathe deeply and read your writing goals out loud.　Read your writing goals, your 3 outrageous goals, your Mother Lode goal.　See them happening, visualize the win, think about how it is going to feel when you achieve them and the difference you are going to make with your book.

(4) **Make sure you are prepared to write**.　Trigger your Writer's Power Tools™.　Take one or two minutes and fire them off 2-3 times.

(5) **Call your coach.**　Sometimes it helps to talk to someone.　If you have a Writing Coach, call them.　If you don't have one, speak with another writer, a friend who inspires you, or someone you admire who can offer encouragement.

(6) **Quiet the "committee" in your head**.　Stop thinking about what you want to write.　Relax, breathe, let your mind wander.　Sit outside for a little while and listen to world around you.　Go to the movies. Listen to a book on tape.

(7) **Switch gears and write something else.**　Take a break from what you are writing.　Think about what inspired you to write this in the first place and write about that.

(8) **Do warm-up exercises**.　Use the Writer's Prompts above to journal for a few minutes and warm up.

(9) **Journal.**　Go to my website and click on www.LifeJournal.com on the resources page and download a free trial version.　You can enter 15 entries for free.　It's fun and it will get you back to that special place.

And then there's my favorite,

<u>Get over it! Just sit down and write!</u>

It's all about your state of mind. Writing is about your state. Your state determines everything you will produce, everything you do.

Dealing with "Writer's Block"

"Just show up – with a pencil!"

Say this out loud: "**<u>There will be no writer's block today, or ever again</u>**". Go ahead, say it out loud, say it with certainty. Keep saying it until you believe it. What is writer's block anyway? It is simply that you don't know what to say. Remember this: *<u>if you can talk, you can write.</u>*

Let me ask you: when you get in your car to go to work or your favorite market, do you get lost? No, of course not. Why not? You know the way. When you decide to make a tuna sandwich, do you end up with a pizza? No. Why not? You know how to make a tuna sandwich.

<u>It's the same thing with writing!!!</u> When you know how to do something, it's always easy!

I will be teaching you five very powerful writing strategies that will show you how to always be able to write and **never** have writer's block. Just like driving to work, going to the market or making a sandwich, you'll be able to get a result very quickly! *(If you can't wait, go to Chapter 8 and read the writing strategy on speedwriting and key words).*

In the meantime, here are some great ways to deal with not knowing what to write:

1. Start talking about your topic. Talk out loud and describe your topic to anyone who will listen. If you are alone, talk to yourself. I recommend turning on your digital recorder. You never know when great stuff is going to come out!

2. Pick three key words that describe your topic. Start writing as fast as you can using these words and don't stop. *(We're going to do an exercise in Chapter 8 that shows you exactly what to do).*

Do as many of the strategies listed on the previous pages to move forward.

Have you found yourself not in the mood? Read your Vision, Outcome and Purpose. Say your Writing Goals out loud. Envision yourself in the future with your published book. Feeling anxious or restless? Change gears. Drink some water, go for a walk, get some air and come back. Call your Writing Coach, a fellow writer, author or friend and talk about how much you enjoy writing and what you are writing about. Ask them for their opinion about your material.

Do as many as it takes to take the next step!

Chapter 6
START WRITING

Deciding What to Write About

Do you know you want to write, but are not sure what to write about? From personal experience, ***the easiest writing comes when you write about what you know***. Write what you are passionate about. If there is no inner emotion, your writing will be dull. That is why you Outcome and Purpose for writing your book is so important, it will determine how much you write and whether or not you complete your book.

Glenn Plaskin, author of <u>Turning Points: Pivotal Moments in the Lives of America's Celebrities</u>, wrote his first book, <u>Horowitz</u>, a 500-page biography, with only the knowledge that he wanted to write. He had never written a book before! But he was passionate about Horowitz, his favorite pianist and hero, and knowledgeable about him. The book was a #1 bestseller! Glenn says, "Write about what you know".

How to Expand on Your Idea

1. Ask questions! Ask lots of "What ifs?" Instead of focusing on try ing to come up with an idea, try this: focus on the topic you want to write about and ask questions about it.

2. Look at books, magazines, newspaper articles, editorials, news stories on TV, columns, brochures, advice columns, financial papers, and, of course, the internet. All of these sources have ideas and information waiting for you.

From my own writing experience and working with people who wanted to write a book, I decided to write an article on how to write. I went to the bookstore looking for something on my subject of "Preparing to Write" or "Getting the Content Out of Your Head". I could not find book that talks about *preparing to write*. Wow! I was so excited!

What started as an article, turned into a workbook that I use in my Writer's Boot Camp, evolved into an e-book and now, a book on Amazon.com and book stores!

Keep Your Writer's Notebook Handy!

> **Whatever you decide to write: <u>Keep an idea journal</u>. When ideas, bits of interesting conversations, great words, little experiences, magic moments happen to you or around you, WRITE THEM DOWN!!!!**

Write ideas, notes, quotes, thoughts and strategies, -- those spur of the moment gold nuggets. I always keep a little spiral notebook in my purse, and as I mentioned earlier, in every room in the house, in my car and I even have one in the refrigerator! You never know when ideas are going to come and you want to be able to write them down – immediately!

I also use this little notebook as a trigger, as one of my visual anchors. I just have to look at it, full of notes and sticky notes and I get energized and excited about writing.

You can use the Idea Worksheet on the next page (or make up your own) to start your Idea Journal. Keep adding to it. You will be amazed at the things that pop into your head!

Have a digital recorder is also a great idea. I use an Olympus DM-20. It is an incredible piece of equipment – small, light, easy to use. It stores up to 45 hours of content – voice and music. You can download your audio files to your computer for listening, transcribing and of course, backup!

You can also convert these audio files in MP3 files and create your own audio CDs. You now have an audio book! You can buy one at www.zipzoomfly.com.

Ideas Worksheet
TOPICS / CATEGORIES / QUESTIONS

Idea	Description

Learning to Write and Being a Writer

Like anything you want to do well, you must practice and you have the proper tools. Writing is no different. If there was a common theme in all the books I have read on writing, and authors and writers I have spoken to about writing, here are the tools for writing.

1. First and foremost, a notebook. You must have a **NOTEBOOK.** This is a must. This is your writing "center." You can be anywhere – at your desk, on an airplane, in a waiting room, at a client site – and all you have to do is open your notebook and there you are. You can write anytime, anywhere.

   You can create your own Writer's Notebook. Buy a 3-ring binder with a pouch for a pen, pencil and Post-it notes, a set of dividers and a 3-hole pouch that will hold papers and items you don't want to punch holes in. This where all your tools will go. Keep your notebook at your writing place and take it with you when you think there may be an opportunity to "take five" and write. You can use this notebook to put your notes, drafts, and completed chapters into. Use a divider for each chapter.

2. Keep a small (3" x 5") spiral notebook or index cards handy – write notes, ideas, titles, quotes, and descriptions of sounds, sights, smells. Be alert, look for details and write them down! You will be surprised, how you can use this material later.

3. A thesaurus, either hardcopy or on your computer. There are several really great online thesauruses. Use your favorite search engine and search for thesaurus, you will get a great list of resources.

4. Act, Think, Work, Breathe, See, Hear and Smell like a Writer! Take on the identity and the physiology of a successful author. That is who you are, at least while you are writing your book!

5. Read! Read! Read! especially books that you want to model. This will give you a basis from which to create your own work. Learn about writing and the process of writing. There on lots of really great books on writing.

6. Start collecting words and build your vocabulary. You can buy vocabulary builders on CDs, through games and just by reading. You can do puzzles and word games. Make it a ritual to learn a new word daily.

7. Journal -- every day! Think of something? Get an aha!? If an idea pops in your head, **WRITE IT DOWN IMMEDIATELY!!!!**

Start Writing!

"When you feel overcome by any passion--when you're in a state of incredible joy or indescribable sorrow or anything in between – write it down. When you miss someone, when you can't wait to share a joke or want to make indelible a peak experience, write it all down--for years pass and memories fade but the power of your writing never will.

You, and those closest to you, can return, again and again, to the page you'll know as an old friend to remember and even relive all that we call the human experience. So pick up your pen or pull out your keyboard and begin."

Glenn Plaskin
Author of Turning Point: Pivotal Moments in the Lives of America's Celebrities and Horowitz

The fastest and easiest way to learn to write is to just start writing! Becoming a better writer takes practice. Every day. Just five minutes a day will increase your ability to express yourself and to create content, stories and characters. Not only will your ability to describe ideas, places, situations improve as you practice each day but this is a great way to warm up.

Just like anything you learn, you start slowly and practice is a must. Did I mention that you need to practice every day? Start with five minutes, then ten minutes and add just a minute or two every few days. It doesn't matter what you write about – just write. Set a timer and stop after five minutes. Do this every day, increasing the time. If you feel like writing longer, do it!

How do you know when you are a writer?

Set up your writing appointments for a week and write every single day, even if it is just for ten minutes. After a week of keeping your writing appointments and writing every day, take a few minutes to reflect on your writing and the progress you made. How does it feel?

Now, don't write for a few days, how does that feel? If you feel like something is missing, you are a writer!

What Can You Write in Just Five Minutes a Day?

As I mentioned earlier, you can write quite a bit in just 5 minutes. Let's find out how much by doing a freewriting exercise. You will be surprised how much you can create in such a short time.

Instructions for freewriting Exercise

1. Prepare yourself to write – in your head, your body, your environment. Say your Power Script, make your Power Move and use your Power Anchors.

2. Select any one of the prompts on the following page and write for five minutes.

3. When you have finished, read what you have written, think about how you feel about your writing (how it felt to write, what you learned, ideas that came to you) and write in your journal about this writing experience.

4. Make a writing appointment for tomorrow for seven minutes. Repeat this exercise daily, each day increasing the time by two to three minutes until you are writing for 30 minutes (or longer!). You can choose your own subjects, of course, or if you would like some additional prompts, go to my website, www.SoYouWant-ToWrite.com and look on the resources page for a set of Writer's Prompts, with my compliments!

Writer's Prompts for Freewriting Exercise:

1. Finish this sentence and write a paragraph: I'm the man / woman / writer / who …

2. Describe the monster under your bed when you were a child. What were the rules for it to stay there? Is it still there? Write about it.

3. Describe a visit to the zoo with a blind person.

4. Write about someone who has overcome a great obstacle in their life and how the experience has made them better.

5. Write a note to a ten year old on loaning money to a friend.

For the Freewriting Exercise, use one of the Writer's Prompts above, take five minutes and write.

_____

_____

_____

_____

_____

_____

_____

_____

_____

_____

_____

_____

_____

_____

_____

_____

_____

_____

_____

_____

_____

Tips to Start Writing for the Brand New Writer

Here are a few quick steps to start writing right now:

1. Decide what you want to write about.

2. Start with a journal. Make a daily writing appointment and keep it. Start with five minutes the first day, maybe six or seven minutes on the second day. Add just a few minutes each day. My magic time is 6:30 am – 8:30am. It started with just five minutes.

3. Use the writer's prompts – you will be amazed at what comes out. Pick a different one each day.

4. After you have been journaling and it comes easily, start by writing a short article or story about something you love and are passionate about – your child, the way your sweetheart kisses you, the shiny new sports car sitting in your driveway. No structure, no worries about spelling and punctuation – just write! *Write the way you talk.*

5. Try talking your article or story. Record yourself telling the story. Find a nice quiet place and start talking. Talk like you are telling the story to a friend. Don't worry about getting it right – just tell it. And if you get ideas mid-sentence, great! Tuck them in.

6. Sign up for a writing contest! They usually require a registration fee and they have a deadline. Two very real things to give you an incentive.

7. Make and keep your writing appointments and you will write your book!

Chapter 7

ORGANIZING AND CAPTURING YOUR CONTENT

If you already have plenty of content and know what you want to write in your book, this is the chapter for you. The next two steps in the book writing process are organizing your materials and capturing your content.

Organizing Your Materials

Let's talk about organizing the material you already have. Yes, this is where you pull out that shoebox full of notes, journals, papers, folders, newspaper clippings, all the "book stuff" you have been accumulating until now.

Use the following steps to organize your material:

1. Get all your "book stuff" out. Materials, notes, research, photographs, articles, letters, Post-its, videos, CDs, memorabilia – everything that has anything to do with your book. This is it, get it all out.

2. Go through everything and separate items into "subject" piles, each pile representing a subject or **chapter** in your book. These are the top 10 main subjects of your book. Put the subject piles in sequence, starting with Chapter 1 (or the first subject of your book), then the next pile, Chapter 2, etc.

This is a great process for two reasons: (a) it gets you associated to your book and excited about your project and (b) you will see how much material you have on each subject. This step will also assist you greatly in creating your Manuscript Grid™ and storyboard, which we will be covering in Chapter 8.

4. Create your Writer's Notebook. Purchase a binder, a set of dividers with 12-15 tabs (depending on how many chapters you have) and insert your material, Post-its and all, into the notebook, using a different tab for each chapter. You can put items that you do not want to 3-hole punch into pocket dividers in your binder.

5. Get your Writing Calendar out and make writing appointments!!! This is it! You are going to start writing your book!

Using the steps above to organize your material will come in handy when it's time to create your book's Manuscript Grid™ and storyboard.

Capturing Your Content

Once you have organized your materials, the next step is to create your content. There are a variety of ways to get your content from out of your head and on to the paper.

Writing by Hand

Many authors write by hand onto a yellow tablet or journal. When I am brainstorming or writing down ideas, I prefer to write on a pad of paper because I use the written notes later as a Power Anchor. When I know what I want to write I prefer the computer simply because I can type a lot faster than I can write by hand. What is more comfortable, productive and satisfying for you?

Using a Computer

This is a quick method of capturing content, especially if you are a good typist. It's easy to edit and insert text. Some writers feel it inhibits them. Do what feels best for you. I typically type on my laptop; however, sometimes I just feel like writing so I grab my spiral notebook and go outside and let it flow.

Talking Your Book

Recording is really the fastest and best way to capture content, especially if you are a speaker, consultant, trainer, teacher or coach. Why? Because you already know your material. If you are a speaker or do presentations for groups, I am sure you have had the experience of walking off stage after a presentation and asking yourself, "Wow! Where did that come from?" I know exactly where that came from, *your creative zone*. I provide you will step-by-step instructions for talking your book in Chapter 9.

Using a Digital Recorder vs. Cassette Recorder

I highly recommend using a digital recorder rather than a cassette recorder. Most digital recorders allow you to create separate folders and files which make it very easy to organize your material and later find specific content.

Digital recorders also allow you to upload your audio files to your computer, put them on CD and listen to them. This is a big advantage as it is often difficult to find specific content on a cassette tape unless you have meticulously indexed your cassette recording.

Writing Techniques

<u>When you get an idea while working on your content,</u>
<u>IMMEDIATELY WRITE IT DOWN, type it or talk it!</u>

<u>Do not:</u>

1. Spend time looking for a document to add it to
2. Start searching your outline for the right place to insert
3. Do anything else except: **WRITE IT DOWN** or **TYPE IT!!!**

Write or type your idea or concept anywhere, just keep writing or typing until you're done. Don't answer the phone, don't get up to go to the bathroom, just keep writing, don't stop, keep writing!

When you finish writing or typing your idea:

1. **SAVE YOUR DOCUMENT**
2. Then, drink water, answer the phone, return to whatever you were doing.
3. Insert the text into your outline or an "Additional Material for Book" document

While writing, I have three documents open:

1. The book document *(a Word file containing my book)*
2. The "additional material" document
3. A blank document ready for power bursts and ideas
4. I have my storyboard taped to the wall where I can see it from my computer

When I am working in my book document file and get an idea, I immediately press CTRL + N to get a blank screen (this creates a new document in MS Word), I begin typing away as fast as I can and capture all the content that comes. I then save it and insert it into my "additional material" document. This provides me with a way to capture new material immediately. I'll insert the new material into the book document later so that I don't break the momentum of what I am writing.

It's important to write ideas down as soon as you get them for several reasons:

1) If you wait, you will forget the idea, or most of it.

2) If you just write a few words about the idea and return to your work, you lose the opportunity of that creative "burst."

3) Writing it down immediately keeps you in that aha! state, so you can keep writing and elaborating on your idea.

Sitting Down to Write

Prepare. Relax and just start writing. As you have your storyboard (a visual layout of your book) in front of you, you know exactly what you are going to write about. Look at the key words and talk about them and answer any questions that a reader would want to ask. Close your eyes and visualize the scene. Bring the key words into your mind and start writing.

Write How You Talk

Write how you talk. It will come out naturally. Don't worry about sentence structure and punctuation – you can edit later.

Keep the Momentum Going

Remember, when you sit down to write, don't start at the beginning. Pick up where you left off. Stop writing for the day at a great place, not when you are stuck. Before you write, be sure to prepare! Read your outcome and purpose. Have it somewhere you can see it.

The Magic of "What Happens Next?"

When you are writing, keep asking "what happens next?" And keep writing! Ask, "and then what happened?" And keep writing. Keep asking and writing.

Asking Questions

Another great tool for creating content is to ask yourself questions about your subject:

★ Why   Why would the reader want to know this?
               Why is this important?

★ When   When is this information necessary?

★ Where   Where is this information needed?

★ Who   Who needs this? Who can benefit?

★ How   How is this used? How will it make a difference?

★ Benefits   What benefits will the reader receive?

★ Results   What results will the reader achieve?

After you ask the question, answer it! Write everything that comes to mind. If ideas are coming to you so fast you can't type them all, just type or write key words, or pick up your digital recorder and start talking!

Research

When should I research? How much research should I do? This is a common question. I have found that if you are writing a self-help or how-to book, write the book first, then research it. I know this may sound backwards, but it works. When you create your Manuscript Grid™ in Chapter 8, you will see exactly what you need to research. Use the Manuscript Grid™ to write what you already know about, and when you are done, you will be able to determine exactly what you need to research. Research only what you need.

Here are a couple of my research strategies:

- My favorite way to do research is to ask an expert. Invite them out for a cup of coffee or take them to lunch. They love to talk about their work.

- Go to the library or bookstore and get ten books on your topic. Look through the table of contents of each book and pull the topics you are interested in. Read what they have to say and take notes or buy a few books on your subject. This accomplishes several things:

    You learn more about your subject
    You get ideas and knowledge to write your own material
    It turns on the creativity
    More knowledge makes you a better expert

- Go to the non-fiction section in the children's area of a library or bookstore. You will be amazed – there are hundreds of easy-to-understand books on a huge variety of subjects. This is a great resource to get ideas for your main subjects.

- Use the internet to read and learn more about your subject. There are so many great search engines, including Google, Yahoo and MSN.

- You can capture your research using handwritten or typed notes, index cards or making a list of key points. Separate by subject and put in your Writer's Notebook with your book materials.

Developing A Technology

As you are writing your book, create a "technology" for your subject. This is a great way to create curiosity about your subject and ask even more and better questions about your material. Here's what I mean.

If you are a speaker, trainer, teacher, CEO, leader, specialist, or anyone who has created a system or process, you can develop your own "technology." What is your specialty? What do your readers want to know? What are the steps to accomplishing it? **Create an acronym for it**. Pick a key word in your business or industry and create an acronym for it. You are now the founder of the "X" Technology for solving, creating, overcoming "(your key word)".

This is a big step in making yourself an expert in your field and separating yourself from everyone else.

You become the founder of the X Technology. Develop steps, attach your name to it, and you are the expert. Take existing information and ask, "What else do people want to know about it?" Simplify it and add your name. This is fantastic for How-To books because it creates credibility. A system or process exists for your subject.

I created the Writer's "Power Tools™":

- The Writer's Power Script
- The Writer's Power Move
- The Writer's Power Anchors

I also created the "Writer's Boot Camp", "Manuscript Grid™", "Writer's Calendar" and the "Schedule Your Success" system for writing your book.

These are strategies and techniques that I created and named based on what I had learned from my own research and working with many writers and authors. As I gave these original ideas and concepts my own name, they became my "technology."

Chapter 8

WRITING STRATEGIES FOR CREATING CONTENT

Getting It Out of Your Head

Are you ready to create your book? Here are five book-writing techniques for creating your book and getting the content out of your head and on to the paper. I have used them all and know they work!

★ **Book-Writing Technique #1:** <u>**Speedwriting and Key Words**</u> *(Page 79)* This is a great way to get ideas out of your head and onto the paper quickly. Use this strategy for getting the big picture on paper. You will be amazed at how much you can write in just five minutes using this technique.

★ **Book-Writing Technique #2:** <u>**Describe Your Book**</u> *(Page 84)* Complete this fun exercise to visualize and describe your book! When you are done, you will have a powerful tool to create three important components to use with your book.

★ **Book-Writing Technique #3:** <u>**Manuscript Grid™**</u> *(Page 86)* Use this tool to create a blueprint for your book. You will be able to see your book's structure and layout.

★ **Book-Writing Technique #4:** <u>**Storyboard**</u> *(Page 89)* Watch your book come alive with a Storyboard. Use this technique to create a visual outline of your book. This is a very powerful tool whether you plan to "talk" or write your book.

★ **Book-Writing Technique #5: <u>Chapter Questions</u>** *(Page 94)* Not sure what to say in your book? Use this technique to generate ideas and create content for your book. This is especially powerful for "How-To" books.

Book-Writing Technique #1:
SPEEDWRITING AND KEY WORDS STRATEGY

What Can You Write in Just Five Minutes a Day? That is a great question!

Did you know that if you are given three words, your mind will create a picture, a scene, a story or an image in your mind? Now, imagine taking that image and writing, writing as fast as you can without stopping to think, punctuate or edit. Five minutes of power writing. This is a very effective way to give your imagination free rein to create.

You can use this powerful writing strategy as one of the tools to write your book. It is a fantastic way to produce content quickly. You will be surprised by how much writing you can do in just 5 little minutes!

Are you ready? Here are the rules for the Speedwriting Keywords exercise:

1. Look at the series of key words on the next page.

2. Select one of the series of key words to write about.

3. Set your clock for five minutes.

4. Any one of the three words must start the first sentence.

5. The other two words must appear in the first paragraph

6. Write for five minutes. **Don't think, don't punctuate, don't edit. <u>JUST WRITE</u>. Write as much as you can. Write as fast as you can.** Don't let the pen stop. Let the words come out and just keep writing.

7. Create a story. Keep asking yourself: "What happened next?" and keep writing. Ask again, "And then what happened?" and write more.

8. When your five minutes are up, stop writing.

9. Final instructions:

✓ Look at the series of key words.
✓ Pick one series to write about.
✓ Get the final instruction at the bottom of the page.

Speedwriting Exercise

Key Words

Ring Chapel Cell phone	Puppy Basket Children	Sports Car Groceries Melting Ice Cream
Paris Sunflowers Vineyard	House for Sale Thursday Agent	Music Heart Candles
Shoes Luggage Tickets	Fishing Tackle Lake Tuna Sandwich	Gun Argument Rug
Ocean Vacation Missing Car Keys	Strong Wind Pounding Waves Sea Shell	Dolphin Hungry Yacht
Escape Countryside Motor Cycle	Couple Holding Hands Anniversary Gifts	Piano Wine Glasses Birthday
Abandoned Car Smoke 911	Friends Bar-b-que Uninvited Guest	Palm Tree Beach Bikini
Author Autograph Best-Seller	Writing Fun Amazing	Movies Popcorn Newlyweds

Okay, are you ready? Look at the series you picked, **now take the next series of words** and write! Yes! Go! Take the next series and start writing! **That's right, take the next series and start writing on the next page!** No cheating! Just start writing!

Five Minute Speedwriting Exercise

Keep Asking: What Happened Next? And Keep Writing!

Stop writing at the end of five minutes.

Wasn't that fun? How much did you write? A half-page? Two-thirds of a page? Definitely more than you expected, right? Take a minute and read it. Not bad, I'll bet. Are you amazed at what came out? Are you surprised at how well and how fast you wrote?

Did choosing the next series of key words throw you off? Yes? I did that for a specific reason – so you would not have a story in mind when the 5 minute writing period began. I have conducted this exercise with many of my students and groups and the results are always the same – puzzled looks and amazing results. Why did this work? Why were you able to write so much? Here's why:

1. Three key words will bring an image to your mind – this, by the way, **is the cure for writer's block**! When you find yourself "blocked," conjure up an image and describe it!

2. You were writing for 5 minutes without restraint or inhibition.

3. Your writing was in the moment.

4. You started with a descriptive word, like beach, puppy, smoke, etc., not a boring word, like "the".

5. There was a deadline. Productivity always increases when there is a deadline.

6. As you asked yourself the question, What happened next?, your brain answered and more content came out!

The advantages of using the Speedwriting strategy is that you write in a story fashion and not disjointed thoughts. Another benefit is that for many of us, having a deadline works, the closer we get to a deadline, the more productive we become.

Using this technique, how long would it take to write a book?

Consider the following statistics: Using the Speedwriting technique, in five minutes of concentrated effort, most people typically write 3/4's of a page. Do the math on this, 3/4's of a page in 5 minutes x 4 (20 minutes a day) = 3 pages! 3 pages a day x 5 days a week = 15 pages a week! At this rate, you can see how easy it would be to complete the first draft of your manuscript for a 120 page book in just 8 weeks!

➔ 20 minutes a day x 5 days a week = 8 weeks
➔ 30 minutes a day x 5 days a week = 6 weeks
➔ 40 minutes a day x 5 days a week = 4 weeks

It doesn't have to take a long time to write a book. I love asking people: "How long do you think it would take you to write a book?" I get answers ranging from one week to ten years. It all depends on how motivated the writer is and on how high on the priority list writing a book is.

✓ Charles Dickens wrote *A Christmas Carol* in six weeks

✓ Robert Louis Stevenson wrote *The Strange Tale of Dr. Jekyll and Mr. Hyde* in 72 hours

✓ Sly Stallone wrote the screenplay for "Rocky" in 24 hours.

Also, your book is not about the number of pages. As I mentioned in the Introduction to this book, I frequently get asked, how long does a book have to be? I always answer, as many pages as it takes to deliver your message.

How you can use the "Speedwriting" strategy to create content for your book

★ Trigger your Writer's Power Tools, get in your creative zone and come up with key words to describe each of your chapter subjects and topics in your book.

★ Add these key words to your Manuscript Grid™ and/or put them on your storyboard. *(These are described on the following pages)*

★ Use the Speedwriting technique for 10, 15 and 20 power minutes to create new content. *Be sure to take a break between power sessions!*

★ "Talk" your book using these key words. Get in the zone, focus on the key words, turn on the recorder and start talking!

Book-writing Technique #2:
DESCRIBE YOUR BOOK

To help you prepare for Book Writing Technique #3, Creating Your Storyboard, I have a special bonus later in this chapter with a sweet surprise when you finish. Are you ready? Fill in the following information and answer the questions below:

Author Name: _____

Title of Book: _____

Your Website: _____

List ten words that describe your book: (Example: Innovative, Inspiring, Easy to follow instructions, fun, filled with examples . . . .)

_____ _____

_____ _____

_____ _____

_____ _____

_____ _____

Write two or three sentences that describes what your book is about: (Example: This book teaches the reader . . .; Step-by-Step instructions on how to . . .)

_____

_____

_____

_____

_____

_____

Write two or three sentences that tell why someone should buy your book:

_____

_____

_____

_____

_____

_____

_____

_____

_____

List seven to ten benefits, results or lessons that a reader will learn or get from reading your book:

_____

_____

_____

_____

_____

_____

_____

_____

Perfect! Now you have a powerful tool to create three important components for your book. I'll show you how to create them a little later in this chapter.

Book Writing Technique #3:
MANUSCRIPT GRID™

A Manuscript Grid™ is a visual blueprint of your book. This is a great way to create an outline as you will immediately be able to see the following components of your book:

✓ Chapter Titles and order
✓ Words that describe your book
✓ Topics of each Chapter
✓ Benefits and results the reader will achieve

Take a quick peek on the next page, and you will see a sample Manuscript Grid™. This is a portion of the Manuscript Grid™ I created for this book. You can see how the beginning of the first six chapters of this book are organized.

Here are some of the benefits of creating a Manuscript Grid™ and why it is such an invaluable tool in the process of writing your book. A Manuscript Grid™ :

★ Provides you with an outline of your book. Whether you are going to "talk" your book or write it, you need an outline. This creates the structure of your chapters, their topics and order.

★ Working on your Manuscript Grid™ over a period of days and weeks associates you to your material and content simply by looking at it and reading the key words. This is very powerful. Being associated to your work always results in richer content.

★ This is a great way to prepare to write your book. As you create and work on your Manuscript Grid™, you become intimate with the key words. These are clues to your brain to conjure up everything you know about this topic, to create questions about this topic. When you are ready to write your book, your content will flow easily.

★ Not only provides an outline for your book, but portions of your Manuscript Grid™ can be used to create an outline for various ancillary products: a script for your audio program, an article, a special report or article for a magazine.

★ Once you complete your Manuscript Grid™, you will easily be able to determine how much, if any, research you need to do.

★ Provides you with a very simple way to calendar the preparation of your book. You can assign a Chapter, a topic or a block of topics for each of your writing appointments.

Create your Manuscript Grid™ :

1. If you haven't already, gather all your material, notes, journals, resources, research, photos, etc. that you have for your book.

2. Separate into piles by subject. Put the piles in the order you wish to write about them in your book. Each subject pile will represent a chapter in your book. The first subject pile will be Chapter 1, the next pile Chapter 2 and so forth. Make a note by each pile giving it's Chapter Number and a Chapter Title. This will evolve, of course, as you create your subject piles and begin the process of writing your book.

3. Go through each Chapter pile and put all the material in the order you wish to write about it by topic. Each Chapter is a major **subject** in your book and each subject can have 5-10 **topics**.

4. Using Word, create a table with 10 columns across and 10 rows down. (You can also use an Excel Spreadsheet). Fill in each cell as displayed below:

   Across the Top: Title of your book, Your Name as the Author
   Column 1: Describe Your Book – List the 10 words from your
              "Describe Your Book" exercise on page 84.
   Columns 2-10: Chapter 1 through Chapter 10 Chapter Titles
   Column 11: Lists Benefits and Results a reader will get. Use the ten
   you listed in the Describe Your Book exercise.

Title of Book By: Author's Name							
Describe Your Book	Chapter 1 Getting Started	Chapter 2 Prepare to Write	Chapter 3 Create Power Tools	Chapter 4 Schedule Your Success	Chapter 5 Writing Warm-Ups	Chapter 6 Start Writing!	Benefits and Results
Fun and Easy to Read	Welcome	Getting in the Zone	Writers: Start Your Engines!	Writing Appointment	Tools of the Trade	Being a Writer	Learn how to Prepare to Write Your Book
Step-by-Step Instructions	Writing Srategies	Writer's Identity	Examples of Power Tools	Rule #1	Journaling	Start Writing!	Learn how to Organize Your Materials
Exercises to Integrate Learning	Finding Your Zone	Outcome and Purpose	Create Your Power Tools	Writing Rituals	Writer's Prompts	5 Minutes A Day	Learn how to Create Your Content

If you do not know or haven't decided on the Chapter Title, just fill in the Chapter number. As you begin to fill in the grid, it will come to you.

5. Starting with Chapter 1, go through all your material (notes, journals, photos, memorabilia) in the first pile and create a three-or-four word "key thought" or "phrase" for each topic you want to write about. Key it into your Manuscript Grid™. Create as many as you can, fill in at least 10-15 cells for Chapter 1. *If you have a challenge coming up with a key word, take a look at the Chapter Questions Strategy on page 96.*

6. Continue with Chapter 2 and go through each Chapter pile and create a three or four word "key thought" for every idea, topic and item in your pile. Type in each "key thought" or "key words" into a different cell in your table. This will make it easy to visualize later. Key in all your ideas and key words for content into a cell. You should end up with at least 100 cells filled in, an average of ten topics per chapter.

7. Don't worry if you end up with too many ideas or key words for each chapter, **this is a good thing**. You can always combine ideas, move them to an existing chapter or create a new chapter. This is one of the great things about creating a Manuscript Grid™. You can move ideas and content around from chapter to chapter and "see" how it is going to look.

8. Once you have filled in all the Chapters, read each column and rearrange the key words so they are in the exact order and proper sequence of your book.

Congratulations! This is a major step in seeing your book come alive! You are getting close! Just one more step!

9. The last step in creating your Manuscript Grid™ is to write one sentence (or more) about each topic in each chapter. Write the most important point(s) about each key word or phrase in a sentence. If you would like to write more, do so. This text is going to be your spring board to creating content. It will act as a trigger to remind you of what you want to say about this topic and also act as your prompt when you talk your book.

You did it! You rock! I know this is a lot of work, but you will soon see how valuable these efforts prove to be. You are on your way!!! From here you can take either "talk" your book (which I highly recommend) or actually "write" your book (type or handwrite it). *The steps for these two methods of creating your book are waiting for you in Chapter 9.*

Book-Writing Technique #4: STORYBOARD

A storyboard is a big picture of your book. Creating a storyboard is very similar to creating a Manuscript Grid™ and will give you a roadmap to follow while writing your book. I have created a storyboard with every one of my author clients and the results are exactly the same: a completed book!

What is the difference between the Manuscript Grid™ and the Storyboard?

The Manuscript Grid™ is easy to create. You can print it out, take it anywhere and work on it anytime. It is a fantastic tool to create a book outline because it provides you with a visual of your content and its order. You can immediately see what content is there and what is missing and what research you still need to do. It gets you ready to write – like looking at a map before going on a trip.

The storyboard takes this process several significant steps further. It provides exactly the same benefits as described above but even more powerful because of the way it is created and its continuing impact on your senses. As you build your storyboard and write your Chapter subjects and topics on colorful sticky notes, you will become even more associated to your content. As your will storyboard hang in your special writing place, you will live with it for several days or weeks. You will be able to look at it, read it and soon know what every note means. You can also add pictures or photographs to further inspire you. This becomes a living creation that stimulates your thinking about the subjects and topics in your book, which in turn inspires you to create content. When you are done creating your storyboard, let it simmer for a few days. Look at it and ask yourself, what else do I want to say about that? Come back to it and make any final revisions to it. Make your writer's appointments and begin creating your book.

A storyboard gives you the flexibility to change the order of topics as well as delete and insert additional topics as you are talking your book.

A storyboard makes talking your book very easy as it will keep you in the zone. Using a Manuscript Grid™ to talk your book is difficult as it will interrupt your flow each time you have to look at each of the little squares.

Creating a Storyboard

[Note: If you have already created your Manuscript Grid™, start with Step #4]

1. Gather all your material, notes, journals, resources, research, photos, etc. that you have for your book.

2. Separate into piles by subject. Put the subject piles in the order you wish to write about them in your book. Each subject pile will represent a chapter in your book.

3. Go through each chapter pile and put all the material in the order you wish to write about it.

4. Gather the following supplies: One large piece of butcher or banner paper (30" x 5'), *(you can buy or order online, a roll of "Project Paper" from Office Depot or Staples)* a black felt pen and five pads of sticky notes (3" x 3" work great) in five different colors. Yellow banner paper with bright blue, pink and green sticky notes work great. I will be using these colors for this exercise.

5. Tape the butcher or banner paper onto wall in your writing space. This is your storyboard background. Hanging this somewhere you can see it for a couple of weeks makes it a very powerful tool for creating content.

6. Using your black felt pen, write the title of your book across the top in big letters. Put your name and "Best-Selling Author" underneath it!

7. Take the blue sticky notes and write down the chapter number and title for Chapter 1. For example: Chapter 1 – How to Grow Roses. Do this for each one of your chapter piles using the blue sticky notes. When you are done, you should have 10-12 blue sticky notes:

    Chapter 1 – Title of Your Chapter
    Chapter 2 – Title of Your Chapter
    Chapter 3 – Title of Your Chapter
    Etc.

    If you do not know the title of the chapter at this time, just write the chapter number.

    If you have created your Manuscript Grid™, write it onto sticky notes.

    Stick the blue chapter title sticky notes across the storyboard from left to right as shown in the sample storyboard below. Leave a six- to nine-inch border on the left and right sides of the storyboard paper.

Title of Book
By Your Name, Best Selling Author

Chapter 1 Title	Chapter 2 Title	Chapter 3 Title	Chapter 4 Title	Chapter 5 Title

9. From the "Describe Your Book" exercise you did earlier in this chapter, write the ten words you used to describe your book on the green sticky notes and write the ten benefits or results the reader will get on green sticky notes. Place these notes on your storyboard as follows:

    *   1st Column on the Left: Words that describe your book

    *   Last Column on the Right: Benefits or Results your reader will get from reading your book

Your storyboard should look similar to this:

Word That Describes Your Book	Title of Book **By Your Name, Best Selling Author**			Benefit or Result from Your Book
	Chapter 1 Title	**Chapter 2 Title**	**Chapter 3 Title**	
Word That Describes Your Book				Benefit or Result from Your Book

10. Starting with Chapter 1, go through all your material (notes, journals, photos, memorabilia) in the first pile and create a three-or-four word "key thought" or "phrase" for each topic you want to write about. Write it on a pink sticky note. Write as many as you can, at least 10-15 notes for Chapter 1. *If you have a challenge coming up with a key word, take a look at the Chapter Questions Strategy later in this chapter.*

11. Continue with Chapter 2 and go through each chapter pile and create a three or four word "key thought" on a sticky note for every idea, topic and item in your pile. Use a different color sticky note for each Chapter. This will make it easy to visualize later. Write down all your ideas and key words for content on a sticky note. You should end up with at least 100 sticky notes, an average of ten notes per chapter.

12. Don't worry if you end up with too many sticky notes for each chapter: this is a good thing. You can always combine notes, move to an existing chapter or create a new chapter. This is one of the great things about creating a storyboard. You can move ideas and content around from chapter to chapter and "see" how it is going to look.

13. When you have finished creating your sticky notes for all of your chapters, you should have at least 100 of them. Go to Chapter 1 and stick the sticky notes on the storyboard. Start at the left-hand side and stick them vertically in the order you want to write about them. Do this for each chapter. As the notes go up and the chapters fill in, you can see your storyboard come alive. You can move things from one chapter to another as you work to create the perfect flow.

Here is the structure for a storyboard:

Title of Book Author Name				
Word that describes your book	Chapter 1 Title	Chapter 2 Title	Chapter 3 Title	Chapter 4 Title	Result or Benefit the reader will get
Word that describes your book	Key Word Or Phrase	Key Word Or Phrase	Key Word Or Phrase	Key Word Or Phrase	Result or Benefit the reader will get
Word that describes your book	Key Word Or Phrase	Key Word Or Phrase	Key Word Or Phrase	Key Word Or Phrase	Result or Benefit the reader will get
Word that describes your book	Key Word Or Phrase	Key Word Or Phrase	Key Word Or Phrase	Key Word Or Phrase	Result or Benefit the reader will get

14. When you have finished sticking up the notes for all of your chapters, stand back, relax for a second and take a look at what you have created. Focus on the storyboard taped to your wall. What do you see? **<u>Your book!!!</u>** You have created a visual outline for your book! **Now you can start writing!** This is a huge step forward, you now have the roadmap for your book. You did it!

How you can use the "storyboard" strategy to write your book

Once the storyboard is done, you can start "talking" or writing your book. You have a roadmap to guide you on what to write about and the order to write it in.

★ Each sticky note represents a main point of a chapter or topic of your book. Just go point by point and start "talking" or writing the material on the chapter.

★ Use the "Describe Your Book" notes on the left to inspire you and the "Benefits and Results" notes on the right to confirm you addressed each one of these items.

★ Depending on your content, you may wish to talk or write you book in sequential order, but it is not necessary. Using the storyboard as your guide, you can talk or write your book in ANY order you desire. Just check off the notes when you have completed that topic.

★ Using a storyboard makes it easy to schedule your writing assignments. Make a 30-minute appointment and spend five minutes "talking" or writing (using the speedwriting strategy) on each sticky note.

★ Remember the formula? Schedule your success. Decide when you want to finish your book – 4, 6, 8 weeks – and make your writing appointments!

20 minutes a day x 5 days a week = 8 weeks
30 minutes a day x 5 days a week = 6 weeks
40 minutes a day x 5 days a week = 4 weeks

Book Writing Technique #5:
CHAPTER QUESTIONS STRATEGY

Are you interested in writing a "how-to" or an e-book? Here is a great way to create the structure, outline and content for your book in just a few hours. This strategy can also be used to create the key words for your Manuscript Grid™ and your sticky notes for your storyboard.

Step 1: List the ten main subjects in your book *(Yes, of course you have more, this is your book, you can have as many, or few, subjects as you want!)*

1. _____
2. _____
3. _____
4. _____
5. _____
6. _____
7. _____
8. _____
9. _____
10. _____

Step 2: The above ten subjects are going to be your chapters. Put them in order and give each subject a compelling chapter title

1. Chapter 1 - _____
2. Chapter 2 - _____
3. Chapter 3 - _____
4. Chapter 4 - _____
5. Chapter 5 - _____
6. Chapter 6 - _____
7. Chapter 7 - _____
8. Chapter 8 - _____
9. Chapter 9 - _____
10. Chapter 10 - _____

Step 3: Write ten questions for each chapter that you are going to answer. Put them in the order you are going to answer them. This is going to create the structure for your book. *When you complete this step, you will have an outline for your book.* Use the format below for each of your chapters.

For this step I want to remind you to ask yourself questions about your subject using the following key words: Why? When? Where? Who? How? Benefits? Results?

Chapter 1: _____ (Title)

(What ten questions are you going to answer in this chapter? What ten questions would a reader ask about your subject for this chapter? Make sure to put the questions in a logical or sequential order)

Question #1   _____
Question #2   _____
Question #3   _____
Question #4   _____
Question #5   _____
Question #6   _____
Question #7   _____
Question #8   _____
Question #9   _____
Question #10_____

Continue with Chapter 2 and repeat this process for every chapter in your book. Use the key words to create questions.

Chapter 2: _____ (Title)

Question #1   _____
Question #2   _____
Question #3   _____
Question #4   _____
Question #5   _____
Question #6   _____
Question #7   _____
Question #8   _____
Question #9   _____
Question #10_____

Step 4:   Answer the ten questions for each chapter. You can easily use the "Speedwriting" technique here. Just select three key words for each answer and write for five minutes. _This is going to create the content for your book._   Use the format below to fill in the key words for each answer. Take five minutes for each answer and complete the questions for all of your chapters.

Chapter 1
Answer #1 _____
Answer #2 _____
Answer #3 _____
Answer #4 _____
Answer #5 _____
Answer #6 _____
Answer #7 _____
Answer #8 _____
Answer #9 _____
Question #10 _____

Continue with Chapter 2 and repeat this process for every chapter in your book. Use key words to create answers.

Chapter 2
Answer #1 _____
Answer #2 _____
Answer #3 _____
Answer #4 _____
Answer #5 _____
Answer #6 _____
Answer #7 _____
Answer #8 _____
Answer #9 _____
Question #10 _____

Step 5:   You now have a solid structure for your book. Edit the text so that it flows. You have created your content!

Bonus Strategy: Creating Your Book's Back Cover

Okay, let's put the "Describe Your Book" exercise we did a few pages back to work! Did you do it? If not, do it now, there's a great payoff.

All done? All right, here's the payoff: You have just created the content for three things:

- The back cover of your book

- Your 30 Second elevator pitch

- Your book summary

Here's how to create these three items:

The Back Cover Of Your Book

To create the back cover of your book, you can give this content to your book cover designer or if you want to design your own back cover, here's how.

1. Go to your favorite bookstore and look at as many back book covers as it takes, until you find one you like and wish to model. (You may end up as I did, selecting a component from several books and giving it to a professional book cover designer.)
   Buy the book or make a copy of the back cover, if possible, to use as your sample.

2. Create the format yourself and insert your own content which you wrote above.

3. If you wish to include a photo of yourself on the back cover, be sure to get a professional photograph taken. Unless your book is about bungee jumping, keep that photo of you jumping off the bridge on your desk.

Your 30-Second Elevator Pitch

What is this and why do you need one? **This is your very own book commercial!** From now on, anyone and everyone you meet will get your 30-second elevator pitch. Here are the ingredients:

- ✓ Your name
- ✓ The title of your book
- ✓ What your book is about
- ✓ The benefits or results the reader will get from reading the book

You can create your pitch from the content you wrote in the "Describe Your Book" exercise above. Here's my 30-second pitch:

"My name is Ann McIndoo. I wrote "So, You Want to Write!" It teaches you how to write your book. When you finish reading it, you will be prepared, ready and know how to write your book."

Take your information, write it out and then talk it. See how it sounds. If you get excited about it, great. If you don't get excited saying it, rewrite it and say it again. Practice in front of the mirror. Say it over and over. Now practice with someone else. Repeat it until it comes out naturally and quickly.

Your Book Summary

What is this and why do you need one? Create a short but meaty paragraph about your book using the content from the "Describe Your Book" exercise. Your book summary can be e-mailed, posted, listed, or displayed any-and everywhere you have an opportunity. Have it printed on the back of your business card and use it at the bottom of your signature block in your email signature.

Remember, it is NEVER to early to begin promoting your book.

Chapter 9

WRITING YOUR BOOK

You have now learned how to prepare to write, organize your material for your book and get content out of your head and on to the paper. Now it's time to Schedule Your Success and write your book! There are a couple of items to decide: Are you going to talk or write your book, how much time can you dedicate to this process and what is your desired completion date?

It is important to answer these questions before you actually get started producing content so you can "Schedule Your Success" and stick to your plan. So you can make the right decision for you, let's talk about "talking" your book which is a little different than the traditional method of writing (typing) your book.

Talk Your Book

This is my preferred method of getting a book out of your head, for the following reasons:

- It's very easy, all you need is your storyboard and a digital recorder.

- Talking your book is very powerful because you can get into your creative zone and stay there for long periods of time. For many, especially speakers, consultants, coaches and trainers, it is very similar to presenting, being on stage or coaching. When you are in your zone, all the rich content pours out of you, and because you are not distracted and by typing, editing or spelling errors, your focus remains laser sharp on your storyboard and you can produce much more content.

🖉 Talking your book is many times faster than typing or writing. By simply devoting one hour to talk one chapter a day, you can complete a book with 10 chapters in 10 days.

🖉 This is a very fast and efficient way to get the first draft of your manuscript out of your head and on to the paper in just a few weeks.

Once you have your manuscript, it will be much easier to update and add content to a topic you might have missed.

Are You Ready? Then Get Set! Go!

1. Decide how you will create your book: Are you going to write your book or "talk" (dictate and record) your book?

2. Decide how much time you can devote to creating your book. How many minutes a day? Five minutes a day? 15 minutes? 25 minutes? 40 minutes a day? Pick one. ***Decide and commit!***

3. How many days a week? Three days? Five days? Monday-Friday? Weekends? ***Decide and commit! Make and write down your writing appointments on your calendar.***

4. Decide how soon you want to get your book done and create a plan. Finish reading these instructions for writing your book and then schedule them on the "Schedule Your Success" guide on the next page. Make 3 copies of your success schedule and put one at the front of your Writer's Notebook with all your book materials and notes, one at your writing spot and one at your desk at work where you can see it.

5. The next step is to chunk it down into bite-size pieces. Let's say, for example, you have ten chapters with ten topics in each chapter. Consider "talking" (dictating) your book and commit to spending 50 minutes a day, five days a week (Monday – Friday) working on it. Plan to spend five minutes talking about each of the topics in each Chapter. It may not seem like a lot, but five minutes is a long time to talk about one topic. Using this schedule you will complete your book in two weeks.

6. If you find that you are spending more (or less) than five minutes on each topic, that's fine. This is just a guide. My experience has been 4-6 minutes of talking on each topic. You may also find that you spend 2-3 minutes on one topic and then 15 minutes on another. This is normal.

7. *Use your Writer's Power Tools to get in a powerful and creative state and use these "golden minutes" to talk your best content. Don't worry about how it comes out, you can always edit later. Just talk! <u>Breathe deep, focus on the gift you wish to share and talk!</u>*

8. *Keep your writing appointments* and stay on schedule to complete each chapter as planned. Once you have talked your book, have it transcribed and celebrate!

Schedule Your Success!

Success Schedule for _____ **(Book title)**

By _____ **, Author**

Step 1 – Let's Get Started   Start Date _____
        Writer's Identity, Outcome and Purpose **Completion Date** _____
        And Writing Goals
        Read **So You Want to Write!**
        Chapters 1-2 and do all exercises!

Step 2 – Prepare to Write   Start Date _____
        Create Your Writer's Power Tool   **Completion Date** _____
        Read Chapters 3-5 and do all exercises!

Step 3 – Schedule Your Success   Start Date _____
        Decide & Commit to # of weeks   **Completion Date** _____
        Set up Writing Appointments
        Read chapters 6-7 and do all exercises!

Step 4 - Organize Your Materials   Start Date _____
        Create Your Book Chapters and   **Completion Date** _____
        Manuscript Grid™ - See Your book
        come alive! Read Chapters 8-9
        Select Your Writing Strategy

Step 5 – Get Your book Out of Your Head!   Start Date _____
        Talk or Write Your Book   **Completion Date** _____
        If recorded, have Manuscript prepared
          [Call for Info and pricing]

Chapter 10

EDITING YOUR BOOK

The Editing Process

The biggest, but not necessarily the hardest, part of writing a book, is, of course, writing the book. Once you have finished writing your book, and you've celebrated, it's time to think and plan for the next phase: **Editing.**

Editing, for many people, can be an overwhelming task and in some cases, the editing process can take longer than writing the book! Use the steps below to review the content in your book and assist you in the editing process:

1. **Print your book**. Look it over and savor the feeling of seeing your book alive. You did it! Celebrate and tell everyone you have completed writing your book!

2. **Make a writing appointment with yourself to read your book in its entirety**. I recommend one or two sessions (or as many as it takes) when you can relax and have totally uninterrupted time. This is a special event – enjoy it.

3. **Read your book without making any changes**. This is important: just read it through **WITHOUT EDITING IT.** If you get an idea, think of a better way to say it or want to add text, **just write the key words on a sticky note, stick it to the page and KEEP READING.** This may be difficult to do, but keep on reading. Avoid the temptation to start editing and changing text. This first reading is just to give you an overview and refresh your memory of what you have said in your book.

If you don't read it through first, here's what happens: you begin reading, get an idea, spend half an hour or more inserting new text and then you bump into this same idea ten pages later! *Make your time count!* Take it from someone who has edited many books! **Do not edit** on the first readthrough – just make notes.

4. **Decide How Much Time You can Devote to Editing.** After you have read your book the first time, you will have an idea how much more content you want to add, delete, shift and rewrite. At this point, decide how much time each day, and how many days each week, you can devote to the process of editing your book.

When deciding, **be honest and realistic about how much time you can and want to devote to editing your book.**
Here are some examples:

- Half an hour a day, Monday - Friday @ 6:30 am
- One hour a day, 3 times a week at 8 pm
- Every day at lunch
- 45 minutes before I go to bed every night
- One Chapter a week
- 20 pages a week
- All day on Saturday
- As much time as I can every day

5. **One Bite at a Time.** How do you eat an elephant? One bite at a time! I have found that by chunking the manuscript down and taking just one chapter, half of a chapter or just one section of a chapter at a time, it makes editing easy and doable. This also allows you to focus on this one piece, which results in your best work and gives you a sense of accomplishment.

6. **Create an Editing Routine for Yourself**. Make writing appointments in your calendar and KEEP THEM! This is the most important part -- keep your writing appointment! Remember? No appointments = no book! Yes, the editing part is the hardest (because you want it to be perfect) and typically takes the longest (because it's not as much fun to correct as it is to create). But you are on the home stretch!!! All it is going to take is one final push – keep going!

7. **Schedule the time and prepare!** Start using your Writer's Power Tools! Say your Power Script, Make your Power Move and work in your Writing Environment! Start your appointments on time and work on your manuscript.

8. **Enjoy the Process.** As soon as you start to tire, stop. Don't push. Take a short break and then come back to it, **if you feel like it**. Remember to breathe, take breaks, keep hydrated (keep a bottle of water nearby) and enjoy the process.

9. Each time you start a new writing appointment, START WHERE YOU LEFT OFF. Do not start at the beginning. Keep moving forward, when you finish editing the entire book, you can go back to the beginning.
I have edited many books and I have **NEVER** finished one in one sitting, even when I blocked off several days. This is probably because I am not an editor. I have found that to do a great job, I need to be fresh, inspired and excited about what I am doing. This does not happen when I sit for hours and hours plowing through material.

If you find yourself spending an inordinate amount of time on just one sentence or paragraph, read the content, make the changes that come to you right away and read it again. If you think it still needs work, put a line down the side of the margin or highlight it and move on. Yes, MOVE ON. Know in your heart that the right text will come to you, later. Keep moving forward. That troublesome paragraph will stay in your subconscious and believe it or not, you'll be working on something 5 pages later and poof! It will pop up.

Just keep moving forward, even if it's just one step, one tiny thing a day, keep moving forward.

Remember, just like with the writing, trigger your Writer's Tools and create your magic writing environment. Take breaks, drink lots of water and keep your writing appointments short and sweet so they are fun and you want to come back and do another one!

10. **Celebrate!** Celebrate the completion of each major section or chapter. Let yourself associate great feelings to this process!

11. **Calculate Your Completion Date.** Once you are into your editing routine, you will see how many pages you can do in the time you have set up for yourself and will be able to calculate your completion date. At this point, Schedule Your Success on the Writer's Calendar which follows. **MARK YOUR CALENDAR!** Put your completion date on the calendar with big stars on it and plan a celebration!

12. **<u>Read Your Manuscript Out Loud</u>.** After you have finished your editing (and celebrating), have someone read your manuscript to you out loud. Listen to your book and make notes about any additional changes you may want to make. Do not stop the reader. Listen to it continuously and keep making notes on a printout of your book. **Another way to do this is to record yourself reading the book out loud.** Listening to it will give you a sense of its flow and make you aware of any final revisions you wish to make. Listen to your book, make your changes, and listen to it again.

13. **<u>Get Feedback</u>.** You may also consider sending one or two chapters of your manuscript to different people you know who will read it and give you honest feedback.

And now, my favorite question about editing: How do you know when you are done?

It didn't take me very long to write my book, but a year went by before I finally felt comfortable letting go of the manuscript and submitting it to my publisher. When I finished my manuscript and felt it was ready, I sent it to a professional editor. It was very exciting waiting for it to come back. Even with the suggested revisions, I was happy to make them because I knew it was making my book better.

I then had my book professionally critiqued. Again, like waiting for the results of a big test for several weeks, it was the right move. My reviewer's questions, comments and suggestions prompted some revisions that I would not have thought of and gave me the certainty that I was finally done and my manuscript was now a book.

You'll know when you have finished your book because it will feel done. It's not about the number of pages, it's about your message. Look at the list of the benefits and results you listed on your Manuscript Grid™ and/or storyboard, did you address all those points? Think about when you started this project, what was it that you wanted to say? Then ask yourself, did I say it?

Conclusion

You did it! *Now what?* As I mentioned at the beginning of this book, writing a book can be a great journey. Completing the manuscript for your book is the first step of this journey. Now it's time to think about editing, reviewing, publishing, marketing and promoting your book.

I highly recommend using professionals to assist you with the various phases of editing, publishing, marketing and promoting your book. To keep moving forward, create a Book Action Plan for yourself and follow through. During the process of writing your book, your Vision, Outcome and Purpose may have evolved. Review these and take steps to get you closer to your Vision, Outcome and Purpose for your book.

To Your Writing Success!

Okay, enough reading, let's write! Time to get started! You have the tools and strategies to write, you know how to prepare, so this is it. *It is time to write your book!*

Every journey starts with a first step, and you've taken yours. Now take the next step and the next. Keep moving forward each day by doing just one thing, no matter how small. Do something that will move you forward.

My best wishes to you and to your writing success! I would be delighted to hear about your book writing experience and how this book may have been of assistance.

Good luck! To Your Writing Success!

Ann McIndoo
AnnMcIndoo@aol.com
www.SoYouWantToWrite.com

ABOUT THE AUTHOR

ANN MCINDOO

Author of "So, You Want to Write!"
Creator of the Writer's "Power Tools™"
"Manuscript Grid™", "Schedule Your Success" Book
Writing System and the 3-Day Writer's Boot Camp

Using a unique process she created, in her Writer's Boot Camps, Ann helped new and experienced authors produce 54 books in 2005. She is a writer, speaker and author who loves not only writing, but creating products for authors and speakers.

Known to her friends and clients as "Can Do" McIndoo, Ann has been involved in training, writing and creating learning materials since 1985. When PCs arrived on the scene, Ann started a computer training company, specializing in teaching lawyers and legal secretaries how to use them. Now, many years later, having taught over 15,000 users in 250 companies in the U.S., Canada and the United Kingdom, Ann has taken training and writing to a new level and is now teaching others how to write their own books.

Ann says, "I love seeing my client's face when they see their book come alive -- when they stand back, look at their storyboard and see that their book-writing dream is coming true and it only took a few hours! My outcome for each of my clients is to make their vision for their book become a reality."

TESTIMONIALS

"You did an amazing job – thank you so much!"
Anthony Robbins, www.TonyRobbins.com

"Ann is a miracle! A fast miracle!"
Bob Proctor, www.BobProctor.com

"Unbelieveable! A great process."
Udo Erasmus, Founder, Udo's Oil
www.UdoErasmus.com

"Wow! Wow! Wow! You make it so easy! The material you have created is ABSO-LUTELY AMAZING!!!!! TOP NOTCH!!! YAHOOOOOO!"
Shari Carr, Ph.D
International Mastery Mentor with Anthony Robbins
www.LifeMasteryMentors.com

"Ann, thank you so much for conducting the Writer's Boot Camp. This was the best workshop I have ever attended in my entire life! That's the truth. You are a genius!"
Susan Barnes, Author

"Ann, Thanks for a wonderful weekend. You delivered exactly what you promised and I got exactly what I needed! When I heard about your process, I was skeptical. It had taken me 9 months to write 50 pages of my book. But it's all true. I finished my book during the 3-day boot camp and received incredible training on what to do with my new book. Your enthusiasm, knowledge and clear, step-by-step process enabled me to do what I had been unable to do on my own."
Tim Kelley, Author, Know Your Purpose
www.TranscendantSolutions.com
Writer's Boot Camp, February 2006

"You help people find their voice!"
Shore Slocum, Author

"Ann McIndoo is the one to watch in the upcoming years. Her incredible, unique and successful approach to creativity, writing and producing a workable manuscript will undoubtedly catch on as writer's learn and implement her revolutionary techniques to get the job done while enjoying the journey. A highly-recommended book, So You Want To Write, How to Get it Out of Your Head and on to the Paper, will forever change your writing habits and eliminate procrastination at its core! It is time to be a successful author and Ann McIndoo shows you the way step-by-step through her book, seminars and 3-day Writer's Boot Camp available at various locations throughout the United States. Much like Julia Cameron's The Artist's Way unleashed creativity, Ann McIndoo, with her infectious enthusiasm, will bring you to a new place of creative power and productivity."
Jeffrey Bowen, President & Publisher
PubInsider.com & USABookNews.com

"The information you shared was both simple and easy to employ. Your manner of delivery was exciting; you are a genuine gem, with a big heart! You have created a fan club. As our books become best sellers, it will be thanks to your great teaching. Thank you!"
Miki Bell, Atlanta, GA

"Thank you so much for an incredible day. I had been stuck in my writing for what seems like forever. You helped me get off the writing plateau -- as you said, "There is no writer's block." I know that is true. Not only was your workshop incredibly helpful, but your warmth and humor made the day fly by. I knew by 11:00 am that the class was worth it, but by the end of the day, you knocked our socks off! Thank you so much!"
Mimi Peak, Peak Performance Coach
www.PeakExperiencesCoaching.com

"Thank you! I have had an idea for my book for nearly 4 years and have been procrastinating because I did not know where to begin. It was overwhelming and intimidating. In a few short hours you reduced my task into something manageable and something I can actually complete! The strategies you present are simple, yet effective. Everyone who wants to write a successful book should take your course and make it a painless journey!"
Jean Tenuta, Kenosha, WI

"Hooray! The train has finally left the station! My writing train, that is. I have been thinking about writing, taking notes about writing, reading about writing -- I just wasn't doing any writing. Today I wrote!!! I have broken through that formidable brick wall of fear and will not return there again! Thanks, Ann, for making this real for me! It was a great day! Watch for my stuff!"
Jim House, Chino, CA

So, You Want to Write

LIVE EVENTS & PRODUCTS

To help you "Get it Out of Your Head and Onto the Paper"™
www.SoYouWantToWrite.com

So, You Want to Write!

Guide and Workbook. A workbook that teaches you how to write your book! Discover what to do **before** you pick up your pen. Writing tools and exercises that will get the juices flowing, create your Writer's Identity, and guide you to determine your Vision, Outcome and Purpose for your book. Techniques for preparing to write, organizing your material and four simple, yet powerful and effective, strategies for "getting the content out of your head and onto the paper!" Use my storyboard process and "Schedule Your Success" strategy and Write your Book! *You can download right now and start working on your book today!*

So, You Want to Write! Audio Tutorial Program

Guide and Workbook as described above. Storyboard Kit, Writer's Calendar and CD Audio Book. The entire book on CD recorded by Ann McIndoo with step-by-step instructions guiding you through the entire book writing process. Prepare in 7 days, create your book in 3 – Have your completed first draft in 10 days.

So, You Want to Write! Author's Book Package

Guide and Workbook as described above. Storyboard Kit, Writer's Calendar and CD Audio Book. The entire book on CD recorded by Ann McIndoo with step-by-step instructions guiding you through the entire book writing process. With Ann McIndoo's coaching and the items listed below included with this package, you will have your completed and professionally prepared manuscript.

- So, You Want to Write! Guide and Workbook
- Storyboard Kit
- "Schedule Your Success" Writer's Calendar
- So, You Want to Write! Audio CD
- Step-by-Step Instructions to complete your book in 10 days
- Olympus DM-20 Digital Recorder to "Talk Your Book"
- "Schedule Your Success" coaching (4 Sessions with Ann McIndoo)
- Transcription of your audio files
- Light editing, spelling and grammatical cleanup of content
- Your content in a manuscript format delivered to you in Word on CD and via email

Writer's Boot Camp
Write Your Book in 3 Days!

Discover the Author in You and Write Your Book!

Have you ever wanted how to write a book, but didn't know how to get started? Sharpen your pencil and get ready for Ann McIndoo to teach you:

How to Prepare to write - what to do **BEFORE** you pick up your pen!

- How to Organize your material - *turn that pile of notes into a real book!*
- How to Produce content for your book - **start writing!**
- How to stay motivated and deal with procrastination and "writer's block"
- Writing Strategies - simple, effective ways to produce content quickly!
- How to turn a speech into a book, e-book or special report

Ann McIndoo, Author
So, You Want to

In 2005, Ann assisted speakers and other professionals produce 54 books through her Writer's Boot Camp and Author Coaching Program! Many Speakers Produce 2 books at the Writer's Boot Camp! You can Write Your Book too!

3-Day Writer's Boot Camp
*Write Your Book in 1 Weekend!**

★Learn how you can self-publish
★Have your book in your hands in 45 days
★Learn how to make $$$ with your Book

Register online at: www.SoYouWantToWrite.com
Call (760) 771-8940 or email AnnMcIndoo@aol.com

This is a total immersion program for the individual who is serious about writing their book. I will show you how to get the content **out of your head and onto the paper** and write your book!

- 3-Day Writer's Boot Camp: An extraordinary experience and environment to create your book
- *6 Personal Coaching Sessions **before** the event to prepare, 4 **after** to complete your book
- An audio CD of your book – Listen to your book after the event on your way home!
- Transcription of your audio files and **preparation of your book Manuscript**
- Light editing, cleanup and structure of content *(Full Professional Editing Service Available)*

Your Investment: $4995.00 If you are serious about writing your book, this is how to do it in 3 days. Due to the high level of individual coaching and assistance, each event is limited to a very small group of authors.

Call today and reserve your spot!

BOOK IDEAS